PORNISTAN

ADITYA GAUTAM

Illustrations by Vinay Vikram Singh and Devrishi Sharma

Readomania

Readomania Publishing
A division of Kurious Kind Media Private Limited
466, DDA SFS Apartments, Pocket 1, Sector 22, Dwarka,
New Delhi – 110077
books.readomania.com
email: support@readomania.com
Facebook: facebook.com/iamreadomania
Twitter: twitter.com/iamreadomania

First Published in 2018 by Readomania

ISBN: 978-93-858546-8-2

Typeset in Palatino Linotype by Shine Graphics

Printed and bound in India by Thomson Press India Ltd.

Readomania

India has traditionally been the land of storytellers and a lot of us have an inherent skill of creating good plots, good stories and good narrations. With a little encouragement and support, many more authors will be widely read and attain a place in the sun. This is the essence of *Readomania*—an initiative that nurtures emerging stars of the literary world.

It would not be an exaggeration to say that *Readomania* is the talent hunt in fiction. It goes a step beyond by not just identifying the talent but also nurturing it and showcasing it to the world. In the process, we have created a powerhouse of content.

Readomania has four principle interest areas – traditional print publishing, online library of short stories and poetry, literary events and products.

The print publishing works towards delivering good quality content to the readers. We publish good authors in meaningful anthologies, novels and works of narrative non-fiction. Our books stand out for their perspectives, the plots, the language and most importantly their ability to enrich lives.

Take a break, read something nice, write something beautiful. Read our books or visit us at www.readomania.com and enjoy a whole new world of literature.

Dedicated to all those organisations and individuals who are fighting for comprehensive sex

education in Indian schools.

&

The three people to whom I owe everything:
My mother, Mala Joshi Sharma. The talented singer/writer who inspires me every day.

My father, Surender Sharma. The most honest, most helpful man I know.

My sister, Prachi Gautam. You are an exceptional human being. This world needs more people like you.

Pornography: Printed or visual material containing the explicit description or display of sexual organs or activity, intended to stimulate sexual excitement.

INTRODUCTION

This book is not about my opinions on the subject, it is not about judging pornography as good or bad, and it is definitely not about religious or conservative values. This book is about understanding how internet porn impacts our sexuality/kids/relationships through scientific evidence and advice from experts.

Sex is one of the most fundamental of human needs. How sex impacts us humans goes a lot deeper than the actual act of sex; it seeps into every aspect of human life. Work, education, art, culture, everything!

I belong to the first generation of Indians to partake in the sexual revolution this nation is going through, and I am proud of this fact. We are leaving the old taboos and dogmas behind, which is great. But the question is: Who decides what comes next? What will sexuality look like in a sexually liberated India?

My generation and the ones that have followed have had little to no education on sexuality, but we increasingly have more freedom to explore it and have access to this infinite resource called the internet. And on the internet, the one primary source of information about all things sex is—internet porn.

We are either directly or indirectly using internet porn as our primary guide to navigating this new sexual landscape we all find ourselves in.

This book is my journey into understanding how sexuality works, how porn impacts it, and everything else there is to know about sexuality and porn. I was curious to know how porn is impacting our sex lives. And I was especially interested in finding out about the impact of internet porn on our youngsters and kids—the first generation of Indians who are growing up on the internet from the day they are born.

This book is the result of that journey. This is the book I wish I had read many years ago. It will change the way you look at your sexuality, and it will change the way you look at porn. If you are a parent, it will change the way you look at parenting.

This book has 17 chapters. The first 12 chapters are divided into two parts, a short story loosely based on real-life events, followed by an illustration and then the science and research that delve into the topic of the chapter. The last five chapters do not have the short stories.

The short stories do not cover the entire scope of the chapter; they are only meant as an entertaining prologue to the topic of the chapter.

The science and research section of each chapter is told through different voices, only because those voices sound a lot more interesting than my own voice does. Any figures they give and any claims these voices make are backed up by sources at the end of the book.

These voices belong to:

Info dude: He is our everyday dude, the only difference being that he knows a lot of stuff. He thinks practically, and he says it as it is. He is in this book to help; he is here to keep things interesting and relevant. Trust the dude.

Confirmed sceptic: We all have him in our lives and in our heads. Mr Sceptic will give voice to all the scepticism that comes to your mind when reading the book. He might be annoying at times, but his intentions are noble.

The Brain: Is the brain. Our brain is complicated, it is scarcely understood and in it lie the reasons for how our sexuality works. 'The Brain' gives our brain a much-needed voice. Listen carefully, when it speaks.

Cultured prude: Oh we know Sir Culture, don't we? Cultured prude is not necessarily always a man, but usually is. He/she is that omnipresent voice in India which opposes anything that has the word 'sex' in it. This voice is here to give context.

Guest appearances by: *Savita Bhabhi* and *Kamasutra*.

Following are the Indian doctors who have given their in-depth insights in the book:

Dr Sharmila Majumdar: MS Human Sexuality, M.Phil Clinical Psychology, PhD (Behaviour Modification), Super Specialisation in Male and Female Sexual and Mental Health. Awards: Best Female Sexologist in Telangana, Hyderabad; Best Paper Presentation in Female Sexual Dysfunction, Most Promising Female Health Practitioner in Sexology and Psychoanalysis. Based in Hyderabad.

Dr Shwetank Bansal: MBBS, MD – Psychiatry, PDO, C-TMS (Harvard, USA), CCBT Psychiatrist, Neuropsychiatrist, Geriatric Psychiatrist, Addiction Psychiatrist, Psychotherapist, Sexologist, 12 years' experience. Based in Delhi.

Dr Ajay Nihalani: MBBS, MD – Psychiatry, Member of the Royal College of Psychiatrists, United Kingdom (MRC Psych), Psychiatrist, Sexologist, 14 years' experience. Based in Noida, Delhi.

Dr Aastha Sachdeva: Doctor of Psychology, MA (Clinical psychology), Bachelors in education, Counsellor, School Psychologist, Teacher, 10+ years' experience. Based in Noida, Delhi.

Dr Manoj Kumar Sharma: M.Phil – Medical & Social Psychology, PhD, Clinical Psychologist at NDDTC, All India Institute of Medical Sciences, Professor-Researcher at NIMHANS, Doctor at India's first clinic for Technology Addiction. Based in Bangalore.

Dr U. Gauthamadas: MD – Psychiatry, DPM (Psychiatry), MBBS, Diploma in Child Behaviour & Development

Addiction Psychiatrist, Psychiatrist, Geriatric Psychiatrist, Neuropsychiatrist, 33 years' experience (TOI Survey 2017 acknowledged him as the 'Most Trusted Neuro Psychiatrist of the Year'). Based in Chennai.

Dr Paras Shah: MBBS, FAACS (USA) Sexologist, Chief Sexologist of Gujarat Research & Medical Institute, 23 years' experience. Based in Ahmedabad.

Dr Manish Jain: Psychiatrist, MBBS, MD – Psychiatry, Neuropsychiatrist, Sexologist, 15 years' experience. Based in Delhi.

Dr Indranil Saha: MBBS, MD – Psychiatry, DPM (Psychiatry). Neuropsychiatrist, Sexologist, 21 years' experience. Based in Kolkata.

1

The Great Indian Sexual Revolution

'Ting,' my phone buzzed. 'Ting,' it went again. I sulk for a bit, and then get my left hand to do a quick search-and-recover mission outside the blanket. The world outside my warm, dark, safe blanket is cold and unwelcoming. The phone is cold, the screen damp. It tells me I am late for work and that I have a match and a message on Tinder. I put the phone away and try going back to sleep; screw work, no one should have to work on cold days. A match and a message, *han*? A message from the match, hmmm.

I am 29 years old, live in Delhi, and after yet another disastrous attempt at a relationship, I am single. Last night my 20-year-old cousin suggested I make full use of my singledom by getting on Tinder. 'Tinder is the thing, *Bhaiya*; everyone is on it, the ones who are not, are thinking about being on it. Give me your phone, I'll set up your account!' The idea that I can look for potential girlfriends on my phone seems shady as hell; I am anyway not keen on getting into another relationship after the recent disaster. Ten minutes later she hands me my phone saying, 'Get to work, *Bhaiya*, you can thank me later.'

'I am actually not that keen on dating, I need a break from this relationship business, I…'

'Oh my God, *Bhaiya*, stop acting ancient! No one is telling you to be in a freaking relationship; just go out, meet girls, and have some fun. It's Tinder, not shaadi.com for heaven's sake!'

I reach out for my phone again. Inside the blanket, I read through the profile of the girl I have matched with. I don't quite remember swiping right on her, but her face looks very familiar. I swiped a lot late last night, I wasn't sleepy, and this swiping right business was a lot more fun than I had anticipated. There are some beautiful and smart women out there looking for a friend, hook-ups, boyfriend, or 'that special someone'. I go through her profile and confirm my suspicion by typing her name on Facebook. Yup, I knew her alright; she was in my school, a girl I had a massive crush on in the ninth grade.

'What *Bhaiya*? I have matched with school friends, even with guys in my college; what's the problem if she was in your school?' I was on the phone with Choti, and she was yet again making me feel like a 90-year-old fossil.

'Choti, don't you think it's a bit weird? What am I supposed to say to her, she probably thinks I turned into a lonely, desperate loser, looking for girls on Tinder at 29. I got two more matches by the way. What should I do? Chat with all of them or choose one and chat with that one? I mean…'

'*Uff*, stop being weird, will you? Stop acting like this is a big deal. You're just making friends and potentially getting laid, that's it. Talk to all of them, meet all of them, have fun. Anyway, your school crush has already initiated conversation, you should be taking her on a date tonight. Do you know I lost my virginity on Tinder?'

'Choti, Jesus stop! Too much information. Okay, okay, I'll talk to all of them. Bye, I'm hanging up now.'

Newly emboldened, I start a conversation with all my Tinder matches. My school crush responds right away and accepts an offer to catch up that evening over dinner. As I get ready to meet a girl I hadn't seen in 15 years and only swiped upon a few hours ago on a freaking app, I feel my nerves starting to build up. It's a cold January night in Delhi; we had both agreed on Chinese. I enter the restaurant and spot her sitting, staring at her phone. She looks beautiful, her hair falling on the sides of her face, the light from her phone screen making her face glow. She is wearing black-rimmed glasses not too different from the ones she used to in school. Damn, she looks pretty.

We meet like old friends; the awkwardness I was expecting is not there. We talk about the old days, the school, the teachers, the friends.

'You know, I had a crush on you in school. But you always ignored me,' she says. I put my head down on the table and laugh. 'What, why is that funny?'

I tell her how I would stare at her from where I sat in class.

She tells me how her life played out after school. About the two years she spent in London, about this guy she met there and her wedding last year.

'So what happened?' I ask her, a little taken aback with this new information.

'Well, he turned out to be an asshole. I caught him cheating on me only five months after the wedding. He was probably making a fool out of me all along.'

'Oh shit, that must have hurt.'

'Eh, yeah I was depressed and all. I am over him though. This Tinder thing is amazing; I have met some great people on it,' she says with a gentle smile.

'Oh have you? I just downloaded it yesterday. I was feeling a bit stupid about using it, honestly.'

'Why? There is nothing stupid about it. It's a great way to meet new people. Some of the most interesting people I know, I met on dating apps.'

'Wow, seriously?' This girl and these apps, they both are intriguing me more and more. We talk about life and love and heartbreaks and future plans. Time flies by.

'You know, the last few years have convinced me that marriage is obsolete. You are lucky you dodged marriage. Stay away from it.' She tells me.

'Do you really think so? Wouldn't you want to settle down with another guy, ever?'

'Oh yeah, I would, but I just don't see the point in getting married. We could just be together and be happy. There is no need for marriage, is all I'm saying.'

'Oh well, listen, I like you and all, but I think it's too soon to move in together, is all I'm saying,' I wink at her. She laughs out loud.

'Can you imagine having this app when we were young? Can you imagine it being this easy to express your interest in someone? Just swipe right!' She leans on the table with an excited smile.

I smile back. 'Oh yeah, it would have been insane if we had something like this back then. I would have super liked you! I swear I would have.'

'Super liked me and then 20 other girls in our school, he he.'

We laugh and talk and eat. As I drop her home that night, we kiss. Sure, things would have been different if we had Tinder back then, if we had half the things that teenagers have at their disposal these days. Things are different for us now; things are different for everyone now. Makes me wonder about this new India that we are all now living in.

***Sexual Revolution**: The liberalisation of established social and moral attitudes towards sex.*

'I get the breaking of old cultural taboos due to globalisation, the female sexual liberation due to contraceptives and women's rights, the rise in premarital sex due to the increasing marital age...But what I don't understand is why do they have to kiss in public?

Indian Sexual Revolution: The Facts

Cultured prude: India is a holy land of culture and religion, what is this nonsense about a sexual revolution, *han*?

Info dude: Oh, well, if you would be so kind to allow me, Sir Culture:

Let's start with dildos, shall we?

Even though it is illegal to buy or sell them, Indians are going all out on exploring their sexuality through sex toys.

According to a recent research, India contributes 5–10 percent to the Google search for adult products.[1] Do you want to know where these searches are coming from? Of course you do. Well, Mumbai buys the most sex products (no surprise here), followed by Delhi (Delhi'ites are consistently naughtier than they like to portray). But the most significant growth is in Tier-II and Tier-III cities, where sales have increased by 25 percent in the last 12 months.[2]

Let's use this opportunity to discuss state-wise ranking—we Indians love rooting for our states right? In a recent survey (by an online sex store), Maharashtra landed the number 1 spot (the state that's lucky to have Mumbai), followed by Karnataka at number 2 (oooh interesting) and West Bengal at number 3 (those Bongs, showing off their creativity in everything!). This particular survey also found that Punjabi women lead Indian women in the number of sex products bought (hmmm), Telangana men purchased the highest number of man thongs (hmmmmmmmmm), and Assam was deemed as India's 'kinkiest state', as most of their orders contained BDSM products.[3]

Festivals and seasons seem to have a massive impact on the numbers of toys being sold, the sexual kind that is. According to data shared by itspleaZure (a sex-toy store), during the wedding season traffic goes up by more than 80 percent and sales go up by 40 percent[4] (Oh my God, the perfect wedding gift! Why didn't I think of this?).

It turns out that during the nine days of Navratras the fun doesn't stop at dancing in circles; sex stores register spikes in interest during the festival, especially in Gujarat ('Yeah I'm online, ordering a *ghagra choli*, some *dandia* sticks and a dildo, you want something?').

Still, think sex toys aren't big business in India? Well. The sex-toy industry is worth Rs 1,200—1,500 crores right now and is expected to grow to Rs 8,700 crores till 2020. It is estimated that almost 100 million Indians will be interested in sex toys in the coming years.

Cultured prude: Holy cow! Why can't we just stick to regular toys?

Info dude: Oh, I've only just begun, Sir. Let's move on to children, shall we?

Studies done in the past few decades show that kids are losing their virginity at a much younger age. As the average age of puberty goes down to 9–10 years for girls and 10–11 years for boys, the average age for losing virginity too is going down.[5]

Dr speak (*Aastha Sachdeva, Psychiatrist, Child Psychologist*): Yes, in my 12 years' experience I have seen a shift in the age at which kids are getting sexually active. Qualitatively through talking to adults as well as kids, and through my counselling experience, I have come across a decrease in the age at which kids are getting sexually active. Girls are also menstruating at an earlier age these days.

Info dude: We all know how contraceptive pills had played a big part in the sexual revolution of the west. Well, according to recently released data, India's market for emergency contraceptives has jumped by 88 percent to $104.4 million (Rs 667 crores) between 2009–2014, ranking the country third in the world after the US and China.[5] India at present is among the fastest-growing markets for these contraceptives. More contraceptive = more sex. Simple!

Expert speak (*Ira Trivedi, Author*): All recent data point towards a society that is more open towards sex. Surveys now show that acceptance towards premarital sex has risen dramatically in the past few decades. The Supreme Court of India recently recognised live-in relationships as legitimate. About 35 percent of men and women are openly saying yes to one-night stands. Love matches have risen from just 5 percent of Indian marriages to 30 percent in the past decade. In a survey of five Indian states, 77 percent of unmarried women said they should be able to take their own decisions about marriage. Even arranged marriage has drastically changed form.

Homosexuality is finally coming into its own in this country. Rainbow-coloured festivals and parades are being organised, and thousands of young people in their twenties and early thirties are coming out of the closet. Lesbian groups are budding across the country, even in second-tier cities like Vadodara, Puducherry and Visakhapatnam. The gay social scene is spreading across the country with professional party organisers, a flagrant nightclub culture, house parties and social clubs with names like Desi Dykes and Boyzone springing up everywhere.

Info dude: Till a decade ago, Bollywood movies would not show people kissing. Now we have Sunny Leone, a professional pornstar in our midst as a leading lady. India, a country which was till recently engulfed with shame at even the mention of sex seems to be having what may be called a sexual revolution.

Cultured prude: Blasphemy! But why? Why is this happening to us? Why, why, why?

Info dude: Well Sir Culture, in case you haven't noticed, India is changing.

It is now a young country, with 41 percent of its population below the age of 20 and 65 percent below the age of 35. It is in fact right now the youngest country on the planet.[6]

A study on 'India's Urban Awakening' predicts that 590 million people, about 40 percent of the country's population will live in cities by 2030, and 70 percent of net new employment will occur in cities.[7]

Expert speak (*Ira Trivedi, Author*): The relations between men and women in this country have changed more in the past ten years than they have in the previous three thousand!

More women are working than ever before and becoming financially independent. The prevalence of women in the workplace is 30 percent in metropolitan areas.

According to a recent survey, more than 80 percent of the women surveyed said they wanted top jobs and were prepared to work hard for them. Women's income has also risen contributing to the 'girl power' economy. There has been a huge growth in savings accounts owned by women in the last few years—14 million in 2007 to 29 million in 2011, and also a 78 percent growth in women credit card owners in the previous four years.

Info dude: Not only do we have a lot of young people, we have a lot of young people living in close proximity to each other in crowded cities. And that is leading to some exciting new trends. Old cultural taboos and barriers are getting left behind. Indian women are finally catching up to the west, and a movement towards gender equality has started taking hold in the cities.

Expert speak (*Ira Trivedi, Author*): You see, in the west, sex revolution happened in distinct phases. In India, though, everything is happening at the same time—the change in mindset that the family controls everything, the opening up of opportunities, the relaxation of social barriers, the creation of entertainment options, the easier mingling of sexes, access to birth control....

Info dude: Add to all this a sudden influx of new, cultural influences through cheap internet and a predominantly young population, and we have a country with one chaotic mix of emerging values; we have a country eager to explore-experiment, and we have a country primed for a sexual revolution!

Cultured prude: Okay, so this damn sexual revolution or whatever you want to call it is happening, but what has porn got to do with any of this?

Dr speak (*Manoj Kumar, Psychologist, Bangalore*): There is definitely a sexual revolution happening. The society is now openly talking about sex, and there's a marked openness in terms of its attitude towards sex and relationships.

Unfortunately, sex education in India is non-existent. Most Indians still believe in a lot of myths and are misinformed about sex, and they all resort to pornography for answers.

Dr speak (*Aastha Sachdeva, Psychiatrist, Child Psychologist*): Indian society today is curious about sex, but sadly the information they seek comes mostly from their peer group, like it used to even 500 years ago, and now the internet is also a big source of information.

Dr speak (*Ajay Nigalani, Neuropsychiatrist, Sexologist*): Earlier, most Indians used to get educated about intimate issues through living with joint families, sleeping in the same room, watching others.

Today, everyone has access to smartphones and internet and thus access to pornography.

Info dude: Yup, the internet is where we look for information these days, in fact, we don't even 'look' for information anymore, we 'Google' it. And, do you know what Indians Google when they get curious about sex?

Over the past decade, Google searches for the word 'porn' in India have increased five folds. In 2012, people in New Delhi searched for the word 'porn' at a higher rate than anywhere else in the world (Gooooood Delhi!). A survey by *India Today* showed that 35 percent of Indian women consume porn now as opposed to 13 percent a decade ago.[8]

One self-reporting survey found that 63 percent of the total youth in states such as Haryana reported watching pornography, with 74 percent accessing it on their mobile phones.[9] As the usage of smartphones and internet access in India continues to increase, more people are now easily watching porn in privacy. When mobile data rates were slashed in 2016 due to Jio's free internet bonanza, the viewing of adult content soared by 75 percent.[10]

Analysts and experts claim that 30–70 percent of data browsing revenues for India's communications services providers comes from customers viewing porn.[11] Yes, all those people always staring at their phones, they are not just checking Facebook!

Cultured prude: Whoa! I don't even know what to say. I never thought about all this.

Info dude: I bet you didn't, Sir Culture. Have you ever considered how pornography works in the first place? Or why do we get excited looking at pictures and videos of naked people? Are we the only animals who like looking at nude pictures?

2

Why Porn?

It all started when I was 12, visiting my uncle's house during the summer holidays. They had a son who was older to me by a few years. My cousin was, what we might call, a delinquent. He got me to try my first cigarette when I was 12, facilitated my first taste of alcohol at 13 and was single-handedly responsible in introducing me to the most extraordinary reality a 14-year-old can be inroduced to. He was about to walk me into a world that would change my neurological connections at the most fundamental level. At the time neither one of us had any idea what the word neurological meant; we just wanted to break some rules, have some fun, and explore the unknown.

It was the era of video cassette players. Those lovely, little machines that sucked in a cassette tape at the slightest push and went to work with their hissing and clicking sounds. It was a time when forward and rewind buttons actually meant something, when one cassette meant one movie.

My uncle had recently come back from a work trip to Europe, and he had brought with him a treasure of chocolates, which were locked away in a cabinet, and yes you guessed it, one fine day my cousin found the keys to this ever elusive, locked cabinet. We sat staring at the shiny, gold, silver, white wrappers of the most exotic-shaped chocolates we had ever seen. Some were scattered loose, some sealed in irresistibly delicious-looking boxes or packets, and the smell, that heavenly scent of pure pleasure filled our noses. After having taken in the sight and the smell of the treats, we launched in with both hands. I went for my favourite, the ones with chocolate and nuts (Chocolate with nuts! Is that the work of God or what?).

Me: Hey, don't take those! The chocolate-and-nut ones are my favourite; you know that!

Cousin: So what! They are my favourite too.

Me: No they are not. The mint ones are your favourite.

Cousin: Well those too are my favourite.

While we were busy shoving each other, my cousin suddenly stopped. He gestured for me to look towards one corner inside the cabinet. As I peered inside, I saw it at once, a locker. A locker inside a locker! Bloody hell!

With anticipation-induced adrenalin, my cousin quickly tried out the other keys in the bunch. Click! It swung open. There was a brief moment of hesitation, in that briefest of moments both of us contemplated breaking this invisible barrier that now stood between us and whatever it was that my uncle did not want us to see. Being a locker inside a locker, he absolutely did not want us or anyone else to reach into this safe haven where my cousin's hand was now pulling stuff out from. First came some gold jewellery, which made sense, then a bundle of crisp, foreign currency notes. An evil smile was exchanged between me and my cousin. And then, yes right then, my brother's hand touched something big, rectangular in shape, and light in weight: a video cassette.

What the hell was a video cassette doing inside this most forbidden locker inside a locker? The white strip on one of the sides of its length announced the name of the movie—*The European Fantasy*. With no cover on the cassette, which usually had an image from the movie, there was only one thing we could do to find out more about *The European Fantasy*.

Little push and swoosh, the cassette was being sucked inside the VCR player. A blank, blue TV screen confirmed that the cassette was now ready to be played. A finger gently pressed the play button and…

Passionate moans bellowed out of the TV speakers, naked, entangled, white bodies moved in rhythm, a smooth jazz tune added to the trance of the scene. We were watching white men and women having sex. Actual sex! Those naked bodies, those soft round breasts, that oddly shaped hole between beautiful legs, the primal act of a man humping a woman just like animals do. If there is such a thing as a life-changing moment, then this was it, life freaking changing. With our mouths half open, we sat there, our brains firing strange neurochemicals, making strange new connections, a weird rush of excitement taking over our entire body, while our shorts struggled to withhold the throbbing muscle between our legs. We had taken baby steps into the world of pornographic videos.

> Neurons: 'The fundamental units of the brain and nervous system, the cells responsible for receiving sensory input from the external world, for sending commands to our muscles, and for transforming and relaying the electrical signals. More than that, their interactions define who we are as people.' (University of Queensland[12])

'Yup, minus the tail, they're not that different.'

Why We Watch Porn and How It Fools the Brain

Cultured prude: I must confess, there are times when I stumble upon some dirty pictures, entirely by mistake of course, but when I do see them, I feel peculiar, a little excited, a little aroused. I obviously berate myself and feel guilty about it forever. But…

Info dude: Relax, will you, Sir Culture? I have two words for you—'mirror neurons'. Now, there are a lot of reasons why porn gets us excited, but mirror neurons is easily the coolest sounding of them all, and possibly the most significant.

In the 1980s, research scientist Rizzolatti and his colleagues in Italy were researching specific neuron behaviour in macaque monkeys.

They soon started noticing a surprising trend. When they would pick up any food (a peanut) to be handed to the monkey, some specific neurons would start firing in the monkey's brain. Surprisingly, these same neurons would also fire-up when the monkey itself was grasping that peanut.

The scientists also found that specific neurons were firing up in response to the specific action. The same neurons that fired when the monkey grasped a peanut would also fire only when the scientist grasped a peanut, while neurons that fired up when the monkey put that peanut in his mouth would also fire up when the scientist put a peanut in his own mouth.[13]

The Scientist (*Vilayanur Ramachandran, Neuroscientist, Padma Bhushan awardee*)[14]: There are neurons that will fire when a person performs a specific action. For example, if I reach for and grab an apple, a motor command neuron in the front of my brain will fire. What researchers have found is that a subset of these neurons, about 20 percent, will also fire when I'm looking at somebody else performing the same action.

Info dude: So, mirror neurons make stuff that we are merely watching, feel more real like we are actually doing that thing or that thing is actually being done to us. See where I'm going with this?

Let me introduce you to my friend 'The Brain'. Yes that thing under your skull which starts spinning when you get drunk, pay attention. Brain, explain mirror neurons to these lovely folks, please.

The Brain: Alright, so mirror neurons can fool me. But don't you dare judge me, this capacity of mirror neurons was a massive evolutionary tool, and it still is. My ability to mirror activities and feelings is the reason why you can learn something, by merely watching someone else do it. It is why you can feel pain (empathise) for earthquake victims in a place you have never even heard of, why you watch someone getting their nose broken while boxing and decide never to try that sport, why you make art, why you laugh/cry/get afraid/get excited while watching a movie.

You see, one of my primary goals as your brain is to ensure your survival. It is crucial for you to get hungry when you see or smell food; it makes you more likely to direct your attention towards the goal of eating, which then ensures your survival. So when you see a delicious cake on TV, I get my mirror neurons working, which is what makes you drool as you start imagining that cake in your mouth, you imagine the taste, the smell, vivid details, through mirror neurons. Similarly, it is imperative that you become sexually aroused when you see a potential mate; the survival of the human species has depended on it.

A bunch of researchers in France got some volunteers to watch porn and found that the volume of erections in the volunteers directly correlated with the strength of activation in a part of the brain which is known to display, you guessed it, mirror neuron activity. Interestingly, the activation preceded the response. The mirror neurons fired before the erection even actually happened.[15]

Info dude: And it turns, we humans are not the only ones who let sexual imagery hijack our mirror neuron-driven brain.

In a research, monkeys were given a choice between a bottle of yummy fruit juice and a photograph of a female monkey's bottom. The monkeys chose the photograph over juice! They chose a fantasy over actual food! They chose the promise of sex over food! That is how powerful mirror neurons are![16]

Info dude: Pornography's power comes from the way it tricks our brain into thinking a virtual image is a reality. Pornography offers a man easy access to a willing female (female access to a willing male), and evolution dictates our brain to pay attention to (get aroused by) that image.

Cultured prude: Oh! That explains it. Still blasphemous!

Info dude: Hang on now, there is more to why we watch porn. Have you ever wondered why you can't tickle yourself? Well, check out this fascinating stuff.

The Scientist (*David J. Linden, Neuroscientist*)[17]: We are wired to pay less attention to touch signals that result from our own movements as compared to those that originate in the outside world.

This phenomenon is clearly illustrated in the case of tickling. Most people can't tickle themselves effectively; the sensation from self-tickling is much weaker than that which results from being tickled by another person.

Our brains can tell when our own hand is tickling our body, and reduces how much it feels that tickle accordingly. This makes sense: sensations that come from the outside world are the ones that are most likely to call for our attention because they are potentially threatening or otherwise relevant.

The parallels between self-tickling and masturbation are obvious. In both cases, the neural activity in those parts of the brain that respond to both the sensory and emotional components of touch are suppressed. To intensify the touch-driven signals during masturbation, one can engage in daydreaming fantasy or, even more effectively, one can watch porn.

A study conducted in 1997 confirmed how porn has a much higher arousal response than daydreaming. 'The porno film elicited higher levels of physiological and subjective sexual arousal than was found for fantasy involving similar sexual content,' the study concluded.

Cultured prude: Oh! That explains more of it. Still blasphemous though!

Info dude: Actually, these were the biological reasons of why we watch porn, there are cultural and societal reasons too. Doctor?

Dr speak (*Manoj Kumar, Psychologist, Bangalore*): Humans start getting curious about sexuality early on. Moreover, since in our Indian society talking about sexuality is considered taboo and hence prohibited, kids are bound to get even more curious about it. So one reason why people get attracted to things like pornography is to explore that hidden curiosity. It is a safe and secret way to explore their sexuality and sexual fantasies.

Info dude: Hmmmm.

Dr speak (*Aastha Sachdeva, Psychiatrist, Child Psychologist*): The realisation of self-image or body image starts in pre-adolescent years (adolescence = 10 to 19 years of age). Nowadays it is happening much earlier. This is the realisation that I have a unique body, when adolescents start noticing their own features and compare it with others.

Imaginary audience: A perception starts setting in during adolescent years that people are watching me. These are some of the basic experiences adolescents have, because of which they start developing a curiosity/become adventurous about their looks and the looks of the opposite sex. That's why diseases like anorexia usually start during those years. People who are anorexic have usually been anorexic from when they were 13 or 14 or 15 years old. Because that's the age they get conscious about their own looks and that of the opposite sex, which in turn can get them curious about pornography.

(More about why kids watch porn and how pornography impacts a young mind, in the chapter 'Kids on Porn'.)

Dr speak (*Sharmila Majumdar, Sexologist, Hyderabad*): Viewing pornography is like, if everyone in your city is talking about mangoes, you will get very curious about it and want to go eat it. Peer pressure and curiosity are big factors.

Info dude: Now you know why we watch porn.

Talking of porn, have you heard about that time when *Kamasutra* had an argument with Savita *Bhabhi*?

3

Kamasutra versus Savita *Bhabhi*

It's summer and most of Delhi is scurrying away to the mountains. And me? I was heading to the desert, chasing the heat wave, riding it to the hottest part of India. My parents had been adamant, friends had laughed; annoyed with the whole situation, I sat in the air-conditioned train peering out from the tinted window, with a smile on my face. We had crossed Jaipur, and the dry landscape outside had started bringing back memories—memories from those years when I loved coming to my *Nani*'s house. It had been a routine for many years; every summer holiday I would be sent to live in a small town of Rajasthan, and for some odd reason, I don't remember ever worrying about the heat back then. I had friends, games, and *Nani*'s bedside stories waiting for me every summer, and the amazing dishes she would cook for me. Then one year I ended up going to a summer camp with my school instead, and then the next year the family went to the mountains, and just like that, summer holidays with *Nani* never came up again. Till now.

The decrepit, old house looked exactly the same; it's like it had aged to a point and then decided to stop.

The town was no different, one of those Indian towns that never got touched by development, except for some sad attempts at building roads and shabby general stores selling the latest brands of cola and chips. *Nani*'s excitement at having me over and her exceptional cooking skills had stayed the same too. My stomach bloated from the glutinous dinner, my eyelids heavy from sleep, I went and collapsed on my bed. The sound of the door opening woke me up.

'*Oye* Amit, stop sleeping.' It was Vijay, my best 'summer holiday in Nani's house' friend. He was the domestic help's son, and lived in a small room within the house compound. We were of the same age. Vijay and I had spent countless hours mucking about in the village, sneaking out at night to go see the haunted house, playing cricket all day, and of course the daily ritual of choosing our future wives amongst the pretty, village girls.

'Vijay *saale,* you're still alive?' Vijay had grown taller and the bastard had also managed a full-grown stubble.

'Ha ha, of course I am, *Bhai*. I am not even married yet, you want to kill me already? Come come, let's get out of here, it's too early to sleep.'

As we wandered around the village, Vijay updated me with the village news and gossip of the past few years.

'What about you, what is up with you? What happened to the love of your life Payal?' I asked.

'Ha ha, you remember? We kissed last year, almost did *it* as well, almost...But then she stopped talking to me.'

'Oh wow! You almost did it man, that is impressive! I have never almost done anything with any of my childhood crushes. Why did she stop talking?'

'Ah forget it; she is from a big family, so it was never going to work. Forget that *Bhai*, you remember the love of your life, Laila?'

I smiled. Of course I remembered the pretty-face Laila, I remembered wanting to get married to her, it all felt like a lifetime ago though.

'I have been, oh well, let me keep it as a surprise. I will show you your love Laila tomorrow, in a way you have never seen her before,' Vijay said with that naughty look he used to have on his face when we were kids. 'Also, I have some educational books for you. I will give them to you at night. Ha ha ha.'

He handed me some porn magazines that night, magazines that must have seen better days, man-handled perhaps by every single male hand in the town. There were naked, blonde girls with cowboy hats and perfect looking tits hanging on for dear life in the ripped, stained pages. I almost smirked; magazines were ancient, no one I knew had dirty magazines anymore. But seeing Vijay's excitement, I feigned enthusiasm.

'Take it easy on them, don't get too excited. Tomorrow I will take you to see something very special,' he winked and left.

A delicious smell of something being deep-fried woke me up. Pin-drop silence, fresh air, a cosy bed, and the smell of delicious food, why, oh why had I stopped coming to *Nani*'s house?

Vijay forced me outside the house after breakfast. We walked briskly for a bit, because apparently wherever it was that we were going to, the timing was critical. He told me to be very quiet as we ducked under a fence. By the time we sneaked behind someone's house, my curiosity had faded into anxiety. 'There we go, *Bhai*, right here, let's sit right here,' he whispered as we sat down. In front of us was a tiny hole in the wall, through which Vijay was now peeking. On the other side of the hole was an empty bathroom. That's when it hit me. 'Vijay, are we peeking into Laila's bathroom?' I asked, aghast. Vijay responded with a proud smile. Panicked, scared and with my heart pounding like crazy, I did what any self-respecting teenager would do in such a situation...I went along with it.

After sitting quietly in an awkward position for about half an hour, we saw a girl walk into the bathroom. It was Laila! She looked good, although not as pretty as I remembered her looking; she was all grown up now and was more than just a pretty face. We waited as she turned on the tap, shouted something to someone and left the toilet. In came a fat, middle-aged aunty who locked the bathroom door and proceeded to undress. We looked at each other with disgust and scurried away. The next day Vijay tried convincing me to go again, but I was done. In fact, I needed to show him a different, much easier, safer, and a lot more fun way of doing things. So I called him to my room one day.

'Have you ever seen porn?' I asked him.

'*Abey* what were those magazines I showed you? Of course I have seen porn! This town is not that backward, *Bhai*.'

'No, no, not all that. Real porn. Of course, you haven't, you guys don't have internet here. Come here, have a look. I have a huge collection, the biggest among my friends.' I made him sit in front of my laptop, and double clicked on the hidden porn folder. Gigabytes and gigabytes of hot sex, folders after folders announcing the genera of porn, stuff he had never even heard of. Vijay looked stunned, his mouth open, he stared with unblinking eyes as I clicked through the videos, showing him snippets with different types and different numbers of hot women getting done in different ways. At that moment I had more porn on my fingertips than this town had seen in a fucking millennium.

With a look in his eyes which said 'Holy fuck', his lips mouthed the word 'P-O-R-N' as if his mind had for the first time grasped the true meaning of that word. I nodded my head in acknowledgement, yes my friend, yes. This, this is 'PORN'.

(Left) 1000 AD (Khajuraho temple) 'Haan brother, you were right, the five-hour-long walk was worth it, this is so damn sexy!' (Right) 2018

Tube Porn—The Facts

Kamasutra: Me? I am one of the oldest, the most sensual porn there is, my child. I have been exciting people for hundreds and hundreds of years.

It was somewhere between the first and sixth centuries that I was written, back then they called me *Vatsyayana Kamasutram* ('*Vatsyayana's Aphorisms on Love*'). I am a philosophical work on *kama shastra*, or what you might call the 'science of love'.[18] My creators intended for me to be both an exploration of human desire, and a technical guide to pleasing a sexual partner.

I'm sophisticated, ancient porn, and am still read by thousands all over the world.

There has always been plenty of porn where I spawned from. Have you not seen the erotic motifs carved on the lower walls of the thirteenth-century Sun Temple at Konark, Odisha? Or the erotic paintings and nude sculptures in the Ajanta and Ellora caves, made during the fifth to the tenth centuries?[19] And, of course, the best preserved and possibly the most graphic temple art in the small town of Khajuraho in Madhya Pradesh?

Savita *Bhabhi*: Oh hush! Kama, you know nothing. Do you know who is the most popular *bhabhi* on the planet? It's me, honey. My website gets 60 million unique visitors every month, every single month![20]

Times have changed, Kama. You are history, honey. People read you to kill boredom, they read me to get off. You make them laugh, I make them lust.

Kamasutra: Whatever, porn is porn. Men and women still have sex the way they did a thousand years ago, don't they? Nothing has changed, my child.

Info dude: Hey, wait a minute, Mr Kama, what do you mean porn is porn? Hundreds of thousands of people have been working their ass off trying to change porn, improve porn, evolve porn. Porn has been at the forefront of most innovations this past century. How would you compare a movie from the 1950s to watching *Avengers* in 3D in one of those IMAX theatres? Technology these past few decades has completely changed the game. Porn practically runs the bloody internet; you think it does this by coincidence? Today's porn taps into the most fundamental need of the human brain, in the most irresistible way possible, and technology is helping it do exactly that in ways no one could have dreamt of. There is a whole new genetically modified, sexually intensified, visually amplified version of porn; they call it Tube Porn.

Kamasutra: What the hell is Tube Porn?

Savita *Bhabhi*: Oh ho, you know nothing.

Info dude: Let me explain. High-speed internet gave rise to a whole new creature: galleries and galleries of short porn clips, with the hottest few minutes of hardcore videos, streaming in an unending supply. These are called 'tube sites' because they stream like *YouTube* videos. The world of porn has never been the same after this. Look at the numbers:

In 2016, on a single Tube Porn website *Pornhub*, 92 billion videos were watched over the course of 23 billion visits to the site. That's a whopping 64 million visitors per day or 44,000 every minute! Collectively, that's 4.6 billion hours of porn watching stuffed in just one year on just this one Tube Porn website.[21] That's longer than we humans have been on this planet!

Kamasutra: Dear Lord!

Info dude: Yup, dear Lord indeed.

Dr speak (*Dr Manish Jain, Psychiatrist, Delhi*): The accessibility has increased drastically. The kind of variety, the kind of categories we have today has evolved drastically as well, and it simply cannot be compared to the porn from ten years ago. The porn industry itself has been growing exponentially in the last few years.

Dr speak (*Sharmila Majumdar, Sexologist, Hyderabad*): Pornography is as old as a cup of tea, it has always been there, it has got out of hand only because of the advent of devices. Even a villager sitting and rearing cattle is sitting and watching porn on his phone. It's no more just a metropolitan phenomenon; excessive pornography usage is also rampant in rural India now.

The Brain: See the sculptures and erotic tales were nice, they got me excited, but only for a bit; they got boring fairly quickly. Yes, the magazines with hot models were good too, but even there it was me doing most of the imagining, and once the stash got boring, getting hold of new stash always took time, effort and money. The CDs and DVDs took it to the next level; sure they did, but boy, oh boy, did things change when the internet came along. How did things change? Well... Dopamine!

It is my relationship with dopamine that makes today's internet porn (Tube Porn) different. You do know how dopamine controls your life, right?

4

Dopamine, the Drug of Desire

Why do I want it? Why is it that I just can't get enough? Why is it that I'm never really satisfied?

I lay on my bed thinking. Abstract questions are only abstract because people are too busy thinking about dumb shit, another thought I have. It is the abstract where the answers every one of us is seeking lie hidden. 'I want this, how do I get it?' But fucker, why do you want it in the first place?

'Umii, get up you lazy bum, don't you have college?'

Ah, my mom interrupting what could have been yet another life-altering, enlightenment-achieving, literature-worthy line of questioning. 'Why is it, Mom? Why do I get up? Why do I go to college or eat breakfast? Why do you refuse to stop calling me Ummii, what drives this...'

'Oh shoosh, get ready, I've made *aalu ke parathe*.'

College is abuzz; there are loads of new faces, the first-year students, *fucchas* we call them. Eighteen-year-olds, lost, excited, scared, eager to fit in. Ragging is in full swing. I don't care much for embarrassing people, so I sit observing the scene, sharing a cigarette with my best friend, Rahul.

He nudges me, 'Fucker, check out that *fuccha.*' What good is a best friend if he doesn't get you to check out women?

I turn to look at the girl: long hair, petite body, an innocent smile on her pretty face. The kind of girl who could easily be in a movie, the kind of girl you know all men around her are checking out. We call her over; we get her to dance and sing and stuff, because she is pretty and because we can. I am extremely attracted to her, so I go back home that day and think about her while stroking the meat. I see her in college every day, and it makes me want her more and more. I start wanting to be around her, so I find excuses to talk to her, I start wanting to kiss her, have sex with her. Finally, one day I ask her out. The next few months are amazing. I have what I so badly wanted. Long kisses, great sex, lots of teasing, lots of laughs. While I overload on this one want, I do still want other things—I do want to play basketball with my friends, eat yummy kebabs, smoke cigarettes, but not nearly as much as I want that girl.

But, about six months into the relationship I feel a shift happening inside me. I try ignoring it, but it keeps creeping on me, refusing to be ignored.

'Dude, I'm just not attracted to her anymore. I don't find her jokes funny, I don't even find her all that pretty now. It's fucked up. I want to play basketball more than I want to meet her. Actually, I even want to hook up with other girls now,' I confide in Rahul, who responds with hysterical laughter.

Confused, lost, caught in a whirlpool of wanting and not wanting, I finally decide to come clean to my girlfriend. Her reaction is half what I expected and half unexpected. Sure she is surprised and hurt; she even cries, but then she calms down and tells me all about how she has always wanted to make out with my best friend. I am shattered. And suddenly, I want her again.

Why do we want? Why is it that we just can't get enough? Why is it that we're never really satisfied?

Dopamine!

'Okay then, just focus and read the book. Simple.'

The Scicnce behind It

Confirmed Sceptic: Dopamine? Why the hell are you talking about dopamine? We are here to know about porn, isn't it? Anyway, I know all about dopamine, it makes us feel pleasure. There you go.

Info dude: Aaaaaaa nope. Brain'y, would you mind?

The Brain: Sure dude, let me explain. Dopamine is created in various parts of me and is critical in all sorts of functions, including thinking, moving, sleeping, mood setting, attention, motivation, seeking and rewarding.[22]

So what is dopamine? Well, it is a neurotransmitter. Neurotransmitters are the brain chemicals that communicate information throughout our brain and body. So this dopamine controls the reward and pleasure centres inside me. (It does other stuff too, but let's not worry about that for now.)

Dopamine amps up activity in my reward circuitry, and it is this reward circuitry that gets you to do or not do things. The bigger the squirt of dopamine, the bigger a reward I am expecting, and the more I make you want that thing. No dopamine, and you ignore it.

High-calorie chocolate cake and ice cream—a big blast. Celery—not so much! Dopamine surges are the barometer by which I determine the value of any experience. Dopamine tells you what to approach or avoid, and where to put your attention.[23]

Confirmed sceptic: Oh well, just like I said, dopamine gives us pleasure.

The Brain: No, no, Mr Sceptic, dopamine is not about the pleasure, it is about the anticipation of pleasure. It is about the pursuit of happiness rather than happiness itself, see the difference?[24] What makes us feel pleasure is the opioid system inside me, and here is the important part—the dopamine system is much stronger than the opioid system. Evolution, son, evolution. Seeking (dopamine) is more likely to keep you alive than sitting around with a satisfied (opioid) feeling. So I give dopamine a lot more importance.

The dopamine-seeking system inside me is what keeps you motivated to move through your world, learn, and survive. And not just physical needs like food and sex, dopamine is what drives your concepts and ideas. It makes you curious about certain ideas and fuels your search for information. The reason why humans went from hunting in forests to landing on the bloody moon! I am hard-wired to make you seek. Dopamine causes you to want, desire, seek out and search.[25] You know how you always seek more than you are satisfied? How once you achieve something, you instantly start seeking something else? It is all because of dopamine, son.

Info dude: Well done, Brain'y! Let me break this down for these lovely folks. What Brain'y is trying to say is, dopamine is the shit!

Scientists have found that individuals who are more willing to complete tasks in the hope of a reward, have more dopamine activity in the part of their brain which controls motivation.[26] People who can easily work long hours on projects hoping for eventually getting rewarded for it, and people who find it hard to work on things that are 'not fun' right there and then, both have dopamine and their brain's reward system to thank or blame for it.

If a task is producing dopamine in your brain, you will be more motivated to keep doing it. That time when you forced yourself to stay up all night and study before the exam, you could pull that off because your brain was anticipating that this hard work right now will eventually lead to the dopamine hit of getting good grades. That night when you stayed up all night partying, hanging out with friends, without any effort whatsoever, you could do it because your brain was getting dopamine hits throughout the night triggered by drinking/eating/sex/laughing/connecting with friends....

This next research is interesting, and also a bit sadist, which usually makes things fascinating.

During this experiment, researchers treated a mouse so that it could not produce any dopamine. With no dopamine, the mouse did not even walk up to the food that was kept in his cage, and if you know anything about mice, you know they can go to great heights/lengths for food. The mouse could still chew food and digest it, but it just did not see the point in it. It literally starved itself to death. Hence proved—no dopamine, no motivation.[27]

Confirmed sceptic: Alright, alright, I get it. Dopamine is important. What does this have to do with porn again?

Dr speak (*Shwetank Bansal, Neuropsychiatrist, Sexologist*): At a biological level what happens is that, whenever we seek any kind of pleasure, dopamine is being released. When we think of consuming alcohol there is dopamine, when we think of watching pornography, there is dopamine again.

Dr speak (*Kevin Majeres, Behavioural and Cognitive Therapists, Harvard Business School*)[28]: Dopamine is the drug of desire—when you see something desirable, your brain pours out dopamine, saying 'Go for it! Do whatever it takes!'. Dopamine fixes your attention on that desirable object, giving you your power of concentration.

So when someone clicks and sees a new pornographic image, his lower brain thinks this is the real thing (mirror neurons, remember?), this is the lady he must win over with all his might (evolution, remember?), and so he gets an enormous dopamine flood in his upper brain, causing a wild amount of electrical energy.

This exposure to a new female who is a potential mate wasn't something that happened a lot to our ancestors, maybe just only once in their lives; so the brain thinks this is a big deal. It doesn't know that now the game has completely changed.

Info dude: The game has changed alright. These days porn can get dopamine working as nothing else can. When it comes to dopamine, internet porn (Tube Porn) has superpowers, it is freakin' Superman. Let me show you how.

5

What Do Porn and French Fries Have in Common?

The night is dark; the streets deserted, I run towards the screams. Strong, light, big: the black outfit is perfect, the cape swirls behind me. I feel like a superhero; wait a minute, I am a freakin' superhero! I turn into a small alley between red-bricked apartment buildings and it starts raining. The alley is dark, an overflowing dumpster stands in the middle, and I see two men trying to rape a girl at the end of the alley. Shit, this-is-my-superhero moment! I expand my chest, take in a deep breath, a gush of cool wind and everything slows down. The men stand up and point their knives at me, the girl stops screaming and smiles. 'My hero, come save me,' she whispers and blows a kiss. I walk towards them; as I get closer, the men get bigger, much bigger. I stand in front of the giants; they smirk and say, 'What are you going to do, you loser? You can't do anything,' The girl looks a bit worried. I feel a bit worried too thinking what the hell am I supposed to do? Just then I feel a surge of energy building up inside me. It travels up from my stomach to my chest and out it comes. An epic burst of vomit gushes out of me and hits one of the men on the face.

'Hahahahahaha, okay wait, wait, so that's it, your dream ends there, you fucking vomit? Hahahahahaha.'

I am sitting with three friends who are all struggling to breathe as they laugh at my dream's expense. 'Well it was a realistic dream, fuckers, you know, I mean I could actually do that shit.'

'Yeah, sure. Just don't ever use your powers for evil, bro. I wonder what happened to those guys, did they die of the stink, or commit suicide from disgust?' They laugh some more and I laugh with them.

'Talking about realistic powers, I can eat these chips all day every single day; that has to be some sort of superpower, right?' One of them says while munching on a packet of potato chips.

'Well, I can bloody jerk off like ten times a day, does that count?' says another.

'Ten is impressive, but here, I'll give you a superpower. Last night, while you were vomiting on people, I watched porn all night, like five-six hours non-stop, and I could have kept going, only that my maid wanted to clean the room in the morning. Now that is a superpower boys,' says the third friend.

'All night *han*, not bad! I bet I could do that too though, I just haven't tried,' I said, and they seem to agree.

'Yup, I could do it, just give me lots of Uncle Chipps and toilet breaks, I'll do it.'

'I haven't tried it either, I guess if I held back on jerking off I could go on for a while. There is enough porn out there to last our lifetimes.'

'Oh yes, there is more than enough of it, and endless variety too. You could just keep going.'

> ***Stimulus**: Something that can elicit or evoke a physiological response in a cell, a tissue, or an organism.*

'Can I have a BDSM with a topping of MILF and barely legal? Oh ya, could you also add some BBW on the side, please?'

The Science behind It

Confirmed sceptic: French fries and porn? Porn and superpowers? Now you're just losing it. Make some sense, will you?

Info dude: Make sense I will, Mr Sceptic, stay with me. Superstimulus!

Confirmed sceptic: Wait, wait, super what?

Info dude: A superstimulus, my friend. It is an exaggerated version of a stimulus.

The essence of a superstimulus is that an exaggerated imitation of a stimulant can exert a stronger pull than the real thing.

For example, what do you think happens when a songbird finds a dummy egg which is larger and more brightly coloured next to its own smaller, paler egg?

Well, the bird abandons its own pale-blue eggs to hop on the blue, dummy egg with black polka-dots which is so large that the bird constantly slides off and has to climb back on.[29]

Illustration: Priyadarshini Kacker

Here are some more fun examples:

Once a chick hatched, its parents preferred to feed a fake baby-bird beak on a stick if the dummy beak was wider and redder than the real chick's. Male butterflies would ignore a live, receptive female to mount cardboard cylinders with brighter coloured torsos that didn't even need to have wings. And, my favourite—Australian Jewel beetles almost went extinct as they were spending all their time mating with brown, beer bottles which looked a lot bigger and brighter than the female beetles who they completely ignored, until Australian beer companies decided to change the design of the bottles to save the beetles, which they did.[30]

The larger, brighter egg; the wider, redder, dummy beak; the brightly coloured, cardboard butterfly; the beer bottle...they are all superstimulants.

Confirmed sceptic: Alright, very interesting and all, but what's your point?

Info dude: The point is, our human instincts were designed for hunting and gathering on the savannahs of Africa 10,000 years ago. Our modern brain has been unchanged for about 50,000 years.[31] Our present world is incompatible with our ancient instincts because of radical increases in population densities, technological inventions, and other environmental changes. And yes, we humans too are susceptible to superstimulants. In fact, animals encounter superstimulus mostly when experimenters build them, or through Australian beer bottles. We humans can produce them on our own. And we do, a lot of it!

The Brain: Let me jump in. I am ancient as hell, and so is my reward circuitry. My ancient reward circuitry's main objective is to reward behaviour that furthers your survival and helps pass on your genes. Hence any behaviour or activity that has to do with obtaining food and sex = goooood = dopamine (makes us want it, notice it, go after it).

And basically, a superstimulus = exaggerated version of a normal stimulus = super duper amounts of dopamine release![32]

Junk food, for instance, is a superstimulant and is widely recognised as one these days.

Dr speak (*Paul J. Kenny, PhD, Associate Professor of Molecular Therapeutics*)[33]: A new study in rats showed that high-fat, high-calorie foods affect the brain in much the same way as cocaine and heroin.

Doing drugs such as cocaine and eating too much junk food both gradually overload the so-called pleasure centres in the brain.

(Over stimulates them = works as a superstimulus = releases large amounts of dopamine).

Scientist speak (*Nenoir M, Serre F, Cantin L, Ahmed Sh.*): In most mammals, including rats and humans, sweet receptors evolved in ancestral environments poor in sugars. The supernormal stimulation of these receptors by sugar-rich diets (food that is abundant in our modern society), would generate a supernormal reward signal (lots of dopamine) in the brain, with the potential to override self-control mechanisms.

Info dude: Food stimulates our reward circuitry; junk food works as an exaggerated version of that stimulant and hence has an exaggerated effect on our reward circuitry. We have all experienced junk food working as a superstimulus, haven't we? Remember that time when you slammed down a one-litre bottle of soft drink and a bag of salt nibbles, potato chips or crispy, salty French fries without much thought? Now try consuming their caloric equivalent in boiled roots and vegetables. Hah!

Now, porn!

Today's internet porn is laced with supernormal stimulation:

1) Novelty (the quality of being new, original, or unusual): We humans love novelty, it is a strong stimulant. Travelling to new places, eating new kinds of food, buying new clothes (shopping!), getting that new phone (and then the newer version of it six months later), and so on...novelty gets us excited. There are multiple researches showing that novelty triggers dopamine release in our brain.[34] It was an important evolutionary tool in driving our ancestors to explore new environments.[35]

> *In a research, a bunch of people were made to see some erotic content (sexy videos). Repeated display of the film segment (same sexy stuff over and over again) resulted in a progressive decrease in sexual arousal. Replacing the familiar stimulus with new, sexy videos resulted in, you guessed it, bam, the arousal was back in full swing.*[36, 37]

What does this teach us, kids? That when it comes to sexy videos, novelty increases stimulation; the more novelty, the better.

Rule 34!

Rule 34 states: 'If it exists, there is porn of it—no exceptions.' Internet pornography exists about every conceivable topic.

In America, a new porn movie is made every 39 minutes. For every 400 Hollywood movies made, there are 11,000 porn videos made in America alone.[38] Taking into account the rest of the planet and the ease with which anyone with an internet connection can now shoot and upload a porn video, it is a safe estimate that there is literally an endless supply of novel hotties available at a click.

2) Artificially enhances sex: Internet porn offers countless artificially enhanced breasts and Viagra-sustained, gargantuan penises, exaggerated grunts of desire, pill-driving thrusts, double or triple penetration, gang-bangs and other supernormal stimulus scenarios. These work a lot like those brightly coloured cardboard butterflies or the beer bottles, the enhanced body parts and sexual acts get our dopamine firing in all cylinders (the brain sees it as an opportunity to mate with hyper-sexualised individuals).

The appeal of these supernormal stimuli has seeped into our everyday lives. Hypersexualised images are coming at us from all directions, and the need for enhancing the stimulating power of our body parts has skyrocketed around the world, including India.

According to a global survey, India ranks fourth with 9,35,487 cosmetic procedures conducted in 2015, with 'having a good cleavage, being the most common aesthetic endpoint today for the young women'.[39,40] Doctors have even seen a 40 percent increase in demand for penis surgery.[41] Some plastic surgeons in India report a 60 percent increase in patients during Valentine's Day (WTF?). Breast augmentation remained the top choice worldwide.

3) Surprise/Shock: The old school cassettes and magazines just don't compare to today's porn, anyone who has seen both knows this. There is a very good reason why *Playboy* went bust; there is a very good reason why internet porn websites today have 50 different categories of porn. Shock and surprise are a big part of internet porn, and the reason is the same as why porn has novelty and artificially enhanced images, to induce large amounts of dopamine release.

Expert speak (*Gary Wilson, Physiology teacher, Author*): Yesterday's static images cannot compare with today's hi-definition, three-minute videos of people engaging in intense sex. With the pre-internet porn, you always knew what was going to happen next. In contrast, with an endless stream of 'I can't believe what I just saw' videos, your expectations are constantly violated.

Research shows that when it comes to sex, shock, surprise and anxiety all work as superstimulants. In the chapter 'Surprise—Search for a Harder Hit', you can dive deeper into how people are 'shocking' their way to an orgasm.

Confirmed sceptic: Alright, alright, so a lot of sexually curious Indians are watching internet porn, which happens to be much more stimulating than the porn of the past and hence it is getting our brain excited a lot like junk food does, I get it. So what?

Info dude: Well, I'm glad we got this far, Mr Sceptic. You know how cheap and easy access to junk food has had an immense impact on the way we live, our health, our habits, our taste, and possibly a lot more than we are still trying to figure out? Well, internet porn is changing the way we live, the way we love, the way we get entertained, the way we grow up, and a lot more that we are still trying to figure out.

Since pornography is largely playing the part of sex education for millions of Indians, it is prudent that we first take a peek inside the naughty studios of today's porn and find out a little more about what goes on in there, and then inside the bedrooms where it is enacted. Shall we?

6
Faking Orgasms

She was beautiful; she looked especially beautiful right at that moment, standing there smiling in that dark room, a strip of sunlight seeped through the closed curtains, falling on her face and her breasts. I had a hard-on just looking at her; she was mine, all mine to devour. We kissed, her lips were soft, her mouth tasted like strawberries. I was ready to eat her right there and then. I let my tongue venture in, she was a little reluctant, but then she let me explore. We fell on the bed with our mouths locked, kissing, pulling at each other's clothes. I had to get her naked, I wanted to do it, wanted to fuck her. She held my hand as I was pulling off her jeans. 'What?' I asked. She bit her lips and then let my hand go. I smiled and pulled it off as fast as I could. Her red panties were off before she could react, and there she was, all beautiful and naked right in front of me. I got rid of my own clothes and then went to work on making her all wet.

Real sex: I put my fingers in her vagina; she feels all dry and reluctant. I start rubbing it slowly for a few seconds, but since it does not get her wet and she still seems reluctant, I start rubbing more vigorously.

Porn: I put my finger in her vagina; she moans and her head tilts back with pleasure. She starts getting wet;

I start rubbing harder, the harder I rub, the wetter and hornier she gets.

Real sex: She pulls my hand away. 'Come kiss me,' she says. I am surprised, a little shocked even. I lean in and kiss her. This is not bad either, after a few seconds I move down and get working on her beautiful breasts, sucking as hard as I can; this will get her wet, I think. 'Gently please,' she says.

Porn: She is on the verge of an orgasm, so I finger her till she screams. Orgasm number one. Now I divert my attention to her breasts. She holds my head with both her hands and pushes them harder on her breasts. 'Suck them, suck them harder,' she begs.

Real sex: I work on the breasts gently, and then I go down on her. This time I decide to add lip service to the vigorous rubbing; this ought to work, I think. She does seem to like the tongue, so I keep at it, till she finally seems wet. I am all ready to enter her but I am not hard anymore, so she suggests she gives me head. I like the sound of that.

Porn: She screams with ecstasy as I am sucking on her breasts. Orgasm number two. She then pushes me away and starts sucking on my penis like a maniac. I hold her head and push it till she starts to gag; she's loving it!

Real sex: She gently gives me head, smiling and looking shy every now and then. I take her head in my hands and guide it; I push it further and further till she makes a disapproving sound and stops. 'Don't do that,' she says. I am surprised and shocked again. So I let her do her gentle thing for a bit and then suggest we do it. She agrees and I'm finally ready for some serious action.

Porn: She begs me to fuck her, so I oblige and start pounding away. She is screaming her ass off; she moans and comes multiple times. Orgasm numbers three and four. 'Fuck me harder,' she begs and I do. She screams more. Orgasm numbers five and possibly six... we have both lost count by now.

Real sex: I start slowly, she looks lovingly at me, I am filled with love for her as well. She is beautiful. I stare into her eyes, as I get ready to blow her brains out. I start humping fast, faster and harder; she still has that loving look, she is biting her lips. I hump harder, to make her have the hardest orgasm of her life being my only goal. Before I know it I am on the verge of coming, and before she screams, I am screaming. I lay on her for a minute, feeling fulfilled. As I roll off her she leans in and kisses me. I ask her how many orgasms she had. She smiles and ignores the question, so I ask again. 'Maybe next time,' she says gently.

Gonzo Porn: It took the storyline out of adult movies and headed straight for the sex. No longer would we have to fast forward through ten minutes of inept dialogue to get five minutes of sex. They got sex throughout the whole video—*Urban Dictionary*.

'Oh yaa, yes yesss, I'm coming, I'm coming, yaaaa yaaaa yaaaaaa...'

The Science behind It

Pornstar speak (*Charlotte Gross, Pornstar*)[42]: Everything we do is for the people back home that are watching it. Something that looks good...somebody that's sitting watching me doesn't necessarily feel the best for me.

Info dude: Yup, it turns out the sex that they show in most pornographic videos on the internet is, well, it's just not real.

Confirmed sceptic: What? Have you even seen porn? Everyone seems to be having lots of orgasmic fun, ha ha! You know what I mean, they are having fun and they orgasm a lot, so like orgasmic fun, you know like...

Info dude: Stop, please stop, I get it. Here is what 'you' need to get—when it comes to internet porn, nothing is what it appears to be.

Pornstar speak (*Lucie Bee, Pornstar*)[43]: What a lot of people don't realise is that the sex acts you see in porn videos are more reflective of what's physically possible to shoot in a certain location rather than what feels good.

Pornstar speak (*Luc Dean, Pornstar*): In porn, it's all about what looks good on camera. I'll do things on set for the camera, that doesn't actually do anything for me personally. A lot of it is a fantasy that looks good on camera.

Pornstar speak (*Lucie Bee, Pornstar*): I see a lot of porn and think, 'I would not do that in real life'. We're basically thinking, 'How can I use this piece of furniture?'.

Pornstar speak (*Seymore Butts, Porn actor and director with over 100 movies to his credit*)[44]: The porn you see on your computer or TV screens aren't an accurate reflection of what happens in real life. I don't just mean your life; I'm talking about the porn actors creating all that impossible sex you're watching. You're only seeing a small fraction of what really went on.

I create fantasies.

Confirmed sceptic: Damn, are you saying these porn actors are faking those orgasms?

Info dude: They are faking a lot more than just the orgasms.

Pornstar speak (*Tanya Tate, Pornstar*)[45]: Yes, I have worked with some performers whose personal hygiene was a bit poor. I have seen fluffy belly buttons on girls, scabby feet so bad they had to keep their shoes on, and private regions not cleaned properly.

Pornstar speak (*Seymore Butts, Porn actor and director with over 100 movies to his credit*): In my experience, 95 percent of the male performers use some sort of erectile enhancement medication. The ones who do not, generally don't get any work.

My experience tells me that the majority of women are in the porn industry for the money first, followed closely by the adulation, then the freedom, and then the sex.

Some of them don't enjoy any of the sex. Some of them are strictly heterosexual and don't enjoy other girls. Some are lesbians and don't enjoy sex with guys. Some of them find many of the people they are asked to have sex with unattractive.

But they do it anyway. They have learned to fake it.

Pornstar speak (*Samantha Bentley, Pornstar*)[46]: I once worked with a girl whose hygiene was so bad that I wasn't sure if I was going to be able to finish the scene.

Info dude: You know all that back-door action 'your friend' loves watching (wink, wink), well he is not alone. From 2009 to 2015, search volume for anal sex videos skyrocketed by 120 percent.[47] Not only that, a study found that youngsters are much more likely to engage in anal sex these days due to having seen it in porn.[48] But a little peek behind the curtains and things look a lot, mmmm, what's that word, oh yeah, a lot shittier.

Pornstar speak (*Seymore Butts, Porn actor and director with over 100 movies to his credit)*: Sex in porn is designed to look spontaneous, but nothing could be further from the truth. Especially when it comes to anal sex.

Before a scene, female performers have a lot of advance prep, from doing several enemas (you need to make sure that cock she's barely tolerating doesn't unleash a tsunami of fresh shit) to reducing or eliminating food consumption anywhere between 4 to 12 hours before their call time.

Pornstar speak (*Rachel Bernard, Pornstar*)[49]: You get paid extra for anal scenes, about $200–$300 extra. I can use that extra cash.

Pornstar speak (*Charlotte Sartre, Pornstar*)[50]: During my first gangbang, I didn't know some of the things that go into doing anal. So, I like, volcano-ed shit all over everybody. I was very embarrassed and cried in the bathroom.

Pornstar speak (*Tanya Tate, Pornstar*): She tongued deeper, and suddenly the girl doing the licking stopped and screwed up her face. We asked if she was okay, she replied, 'Oh yes, I am now, it was only a bit of poop'.

I gave her my toothbrush and some mouthwash so the girls could carry on.

Info dude: Now obviously not everyone is always shitting on each other in porn (unless its 'Scat porn'—more about that in the chapter 'Surprise'). Actors do have fun, and some of them actually enjoy doing things like anal.

Here is the important part though, the porn industry is not out there trying to educate us on sex; it is out there to make money, the most money they possibly can.

What is driving the industry is not what is 'fun', but what stimulates and 'superstimulates' the viewer's brain. 'How to grab eyeballs' is the name of the game.

There are literally millions of porn websites on the internet competing for our attention (some estimates say there are about 4 million[51]). To compete, they must use those porn superpowers we discussed. They use novelty (new videos being uploaded every minute), they use high-definition cameras with camera angles and expert actors making the sex appear super intense, stimulating as hell, and then they use shock, a lot of it. Shock can also come in the form of violence...

Pornstar speak (*Anthony Hardwood, Pornstar*)[52]: I have seen porn change dramatically since the beginning of my career in 1997 when it simply involved 'making love on a bed'. These days rougher 'Gonzo' porn has left the fringe.

When I started, it was like very lovey-dovey sex, not tough like 'Gonzo'.

Info dude: Some sources claim that about 40 percent of all porn depicts violence against women. Among such trends are forced blow jobs to the point of making girls vomit (called 'facial abuse' in porn lingo). Amongst the most popular categories of porn today, we have rape, punishment, rough sex, forced sex...

Dr speak (*Sharon Mitchell, deals with porn actors*)[53]: I sit there every day and I sew up anal tears and anal prolapse and the physical conditions of what people are putting their bodies through is getting very, very far away from sexuality as we know it.

Pornstar speak (*Anthony Hardwood, Pornstar*): Eventually they wanted to get more energy, make it rougher, so they would do one girl with like four guys and they just take over and destroy her.

Info dude: Again, not all porn is violent and not all violent-looking scenes are being forced upon the female actors. But, by the looks of it, a lot of it is, and it seems to be a growing trend. The reasons behind the growing demand for violent/hardcore porn, and other ways in which porn 'shocks' us is explored in the chapter 'Surprise! (The search for a harder hit)'.

Confirmed sceptic: Well that's a bummer; I mean all that fake stuff. But I guess as long as willing adults are doing what they want to, there is no real problem.

Pornstar speak (*Seymore Butts, Porn actor and director with over 100 movies to his credit)*: The problems start when viewers forget that these are fantasies and lose perspective.

Info dude: Here is the thing though, when it comes to porn, the very mechanism of enjoying it is rooted in us losing perspective. Our brain thinks the sex is real (mirror neurons, remember?). Today's internet pornography with its superstimulants makes the experience of watching porn even more vivid, making us lose ourselves in the experience. The line between fantasy and reality is meant to be blurred, that is the primary goal of today's internet porn.

Research shows that is exactly what is happening:

The findings of a research highlighted a link between porn exposure, young men's sexual expectations and young women's pressure to conform to what is being viewed in the porn.[54]

A study examined 804 adolescent boys and girls, between the ages of 14 to 19 in Italy. The findings showed that active and passive sexual violence and unwanted sex and pornography use were correlated.

Effects of viewing pornographic films on passive, unwanted sex were also found, especially among girls.[55]

A survey done with adolescents (minimum age of 13.5), showed that early exposure to pornography resulted in a less progressive attitude towards gender equality, not only with male viewers, but also female viewers.[56]

No, the ability for porn to seep into real-life sexual behaviour is not restricted to youngsters only.

A research in Sweden showed that 99 percent of men had seen pornography, and 53 percent of them felt that pornography impacted their sexual behaviour and they got inspired by it.[57]

A research done with 833 Dutch adults found that pornography made men more likely to think that women engage in token resistance to sex (i.e. the notion that women say 'no' when they actually intend to have sex).[58]

And no, India is not insulated from this trend of porn seeping into real-life sexual behaviour.

According to an *India Today* survey, 42 percent men and women agreed that watching internet porn has affected their sex life.[59]

Dr speak (*Manoj Kumar, Psychiatrist, Technology Addiction, Bangalore*): I had a case where the husband had started demanding and trying out extreme acts with his wife, which he had seen in porn. The wife was very disturbed by this and was considering separation.

Dr speak (*Ajay Nigalani, Neuropsychiatrist, Sexologist, Delhi*): I see patients who are getting so influenced by porn that it has started affecting their real lives.

Most of the patients I see have expectations from seeing porn that cannot be fulfilled. Such as, 'Sex in porn goes on for 40 minutes, I can only go on for a few minutes.'

Dr speak (*Paras Shah, Sexologist, Ahmedabad*): More often than not people who watch porn start associating it with real life. They feel they should be having sex with more than one woman at a time; they feel they should be lasting as long as the actors last in porn; they feel their penis size should match the actors. Because of all this they develop inferiority complexes. Even women think like this sometimes. They start thinking if a man does not have sex 3–4 times with them, then he either doesn't like her or is having sex elsewhere.

I get many patients suffering from pornography-related problems. I always ask them if they see Bollywood movies, they say yes, so I ask them if an actor jumps from the tenth floor in a movie, will you also go and jump? They say of course not. Then I tell them, exactly, pornography is a movie. It has been edited to look like people are doing it for one hour straight. What you see is just fiction, not reality.

Dr speak (*Shwetank Bansal, Neuropsychiatrist, Sexologist, Delhi*): I get patients who come in with concerns about how long their erection lasts. In porn they are doing it for hours, why am I not able to do that? If you look at WHO's standards, two minutes of intercourse is the world average. But what they see in porn is completely different, which is obviously primarily medication induced.

They come in with concerns regarding sizeand signs of virility, based on what they have seen in porn. It seriously affects their self-image. A lot of people end up having very low esteem because they are always comparing.

It's harmful in itself, but then there are lots of internet portals offering surgeries for increasing size, offering one magic pill or magic cure, to improve the sexual power and all of that. There is a huge market thriving based on such insecurities that are being pushed by pornography.

Expectations, preferences tend to get skewed based on what they are watching. Pornography tends to give a very negative view of women, there is a lot of content that is derogatory to women. What is being seen is that objectification of women can also increase based on what is being depicted in pornography. It can have a huge impact on your psyche.

Real sex versus Porn sex (some facts)[60]

Pornstar penises are 6–9 inches. Real-life penises are 5–7 inches. The average size of the Indian penis is 5.54 inches (ouch!).

While almost all pornstars are pube free, at least 65 percent of all women and 85 percent of men do have pubes (you know who you are, stop hiding).

Real people need 10–12 minutes of foreplay to get going, women can take up to 20 minutes, pornstars are always ready to go, always.

Male porn performers can seemingly hump for days without ejaculating while 75 percent of men ejaculate within three minutes (you know who you are).

All female pornstars seem to have the ability to orgasm through penetration—71 percent of women don't (Your tiny penis does not help. Hah, I kid, I kid! But really it doesn't!).

While most female pornstars seem to be able to squirt, only 6 percent women say that they can.

Info dude: Things start getting extremely interesting when we add porn to the dynamics of an intimate relationship, very, very interesting...

7
Porny Relationships

No time, no past, no future, no job, no bank loans, no bills, no family, no purpose: nothing. I lay on the soft, wet sand, my hands and legs spread out around me, the waves nudging at my feet every few seconds. She stands looking down at me, her silhouette blocking the sun, her hair glowing red, she is the most beautiful thing I have ever seen, a perfect moment, pure bliss, pure love.

We had decided to move in together; the months since had gone by in a flash. We made a perfect couple, always joking around, enjoying the same things and the sex, well let's just say it was constant. We were doing it every day, multiple times every day. It was perfect.

It was all perfect, till that Monday that is. That Monday when she was working late, and I was home alone feeling bored and horny. I hadn't seen it in a while, in fact, this was the longest I remembered not seeing it since school. 'It' had always been my go-to entertainment source, whenever I was bored and horny, or just plain bored. Getting excited about the prospect, I started my laptop, got comfortable, and Googled 'porn'.

The need for gigabytes of stored videos was long gone; the struggle of searching for some good action was obsolete. A laptop, a WiFi connection, a hand—is all that one needed to binge on as much of the good action as one wanted. Few months of being off it and I was greeted by an array of new websites. New had become a constant in the world of porn by now. I scanned through the hundreds of categories, looked at the clock, the next few hours were going to be fun.

Porn was back, in a mellower avatar, nothing close to the intensity of my desperate teen years. I had a girlfriend for God's sake, I was fucking, and porn was just a fun, harmless way to spend some alone time. If you asked me during those days, I would have said that things were still perfect, they really were. Until that other Monday that is, a month later.

She was working late again, and I was entertaining myself again. I was checking out *Brazzers*, a new website with high-definition, hardcore action. These guys were on the cutting edge of porn trends. It was all going as per schedule, I had 30-odd more minutes to browse through videos, and then once I found that perfect one, another half an hour to actually shag, then about 30 minutes to take a shower and hit the bed, all before the girlfriend came back. It's not that I needed to hide anything from her, but it just felt like something I should wrap up before she came home. I didn't want her interrupting my shag more than anything, also I don't think I wanted her to see the kind of stuff that got me off.

Spellbound by the bootys on *Brazzers* and the orgasmic screams blasting through my headphones, I didn't see or hear her coming early, opening the door with her keys, calling out my name, standing right behind me for God knows how long. She finally tapped me on my shoulder.

'Oh baby, what, where, when did you...?'

'Relax tiger, you were too busy watching these big-breasted blondes having sex with, what is it, three-four men?' she said, with a bemused look.

'Oh this...I...haha...I was just...Forget this, just some stupid video link a friend had sent, it's nothing.'

Everything seemed normal that night; we even had sex. But then the questions started: 'Hey baby, tell me something, do big breasts turn you on?'; 'Baby, you know that day you were watching that porn video, do you watch porn often?'; 'Honey, tell me something, does the group sex thing turn you on?'

I dealt with them with whatever answer felt apt at the time. Now that she knew I watched porn 'once in a while', I was a bit more confident watching it often. It seemed as if all had been dealt with again; everything was back to normal. But then, that penultimate Monday happened.

She was working late again, and I was at it again. Streaming that hard-core action and beating that meat. Streaming videos from this new website with some mind-blowing Japanese action; must confess that these Japs are twisted as fuck and twisted always makes for great porn. I was feeling it, so I went ahead and did it a few times. Tired and satisfied, I went to bed. It turned out I was not the only one feeling it that day; she woke me up when she was back, gave me coffee, and started going down on me. She wanted it, and when a girl wants it, she really does want it. I was spent, the meat refused to wake up. Frustrated, but being the sweetheart that she was, she kissed me and told me not to worry about it.

The next day when I woke up, she had that laptop with last night's browsing history open and kept on the dining table.

Her eyes red, her face furious, she screamed, 'You were watching this filthy Japanese shit for two hours? You would rather watch this then have sex with me?'

Now, there was nothing I could say to make her feel better about that situation. So I told her that I loved her. Again and again.

You see, when it comes to porn, especially with some of that good old Japanese stuff, explanations can be complicated.

'Hmm, so why do you think your sex life has been non-existent in the past month? Have you been having fights? Are you both spending too much time at work? Stress? Is it stress?'

'No counsellor, virgin kitties. He got a free, three-month subscription for virginkitties.com'

The Science behind It

Info dude: What did the male prairie vole say to the female prairie vole after sex?

I love you!

A prairie vole is a small vole found in central North America. A vole looks a lot like a cuter, furrier version of a rat. The only reason anyone outside of the central North American prairies would ever get to hear about them is, because these voles fall in love. When two prairie voles mate, a burst of hormones (Oxytocin and

Vasopressin) and neurochemicals (good, old dopamine) rewire their brains into the ability to form intense, exclusive social attachments with a mate, also called pair-bonds (also called falling in love). Prairie vole couples mate and affiliate exclusively with each other, share nests, and even raise their offspring together.[61]

Pair bonding/monogamous behaviour is rare in nature, and especially rare in us mammals. In fact, only 3 percent mammals show signs of pair bonding.[62] We humans happen to be one of them.

Evidence so far suggests a lot of commonalities between how prairie voles pair bond and how we humans do.

Prairie vole sex, for instance, involves an unusual amount of vaginal stimulation—a behaviour that triggers the release of the hormone oxytocin normally associated with childbirth. Instead of bonding with a baby, the female bonds with her partner. The voles' brains are rigged to associate the reward of sex with the presence of a particular partner.

The human face-to-face mating style (good, old missionary position and also woman on top), which highlights a partner's unique physical features at the moment of reward (dopamine released during sex), probably also serves to cement a pleasurable connection with a single individual.

There are many other special ranges of subconscious signals, or 'bonding behaviours' that we and other mammals like the voles and Tamarin monkeys indulge in.[63]

Most pair bonders seem to have evolved this mating strategy because their offspring do better with two caregivers. Humans, for example, take a long time to mature, so parents who bond long enough to allow bonding with children are good insurance.

Dr speak (*Ajay Nigalani, Neuropsychiatrist, Sexologist, Delhi*): Is there a particular reason why a monogamous, straight relationship is the norm all over the world? I think there is something in us that wants us to belong to an individual, belong to a relationship, belong to a family.

Cultured prude: Lovely. How lovely are these mammals, monogamous for life, cultured as hell. Fantastic!

Info dude: Oh before you get carried away, Sir Culture and the rest of you romantics, this pair-bond is a delicate thing, a little disturbance in its balance and all of these 3 percent mammals tend to stray (cheat) on their partners (You know who you are, you innocent-looking prairie vole you!). You see evolution really doesn't like monogamy much. It tolerates it grudgingly in relatively few species.

Our brain loves novelty (an essential ingredient of a superstimulus, remember?). So every time there is potential for a sexual encounter with a new (novel) mate, there is the release of dopamine. Hence, 'the Coolidge effect'…

One fine sunny day, the then US President Calvin Coolidge and his wife were touring a farm. While the president was elsewhere, the farmer proudly showed Mrs Coolidge a rooster that could copulate with hens all day long, day after day. Mrs Coolidge coyly suggested that the farmer tell that to President Coolidge (hah), which the farmer did. The President thought for a moment and then enquired, 'With the same hen?' 'No,

Sir,' replied the farmer. 'Tell that to Mrs Coolidge,' retorted the President (haaaah).

The Coolidge effect is a graphic example of how unrelentingly sexual novelty can drive behaviour. The effect shows up in mammals ranging from rams to rats, and here's how it works: drop a male rat into a cage with a receptive female rat. First, you see a frenzy of copulation. Then, progressively, the male tires of that particular female. Even if she wants more, he has had enough. However, replace the original female with a fresh one, and the male immediately revives and gallantly struggles to fertilise her. You can repeat this process with fresh females until he is completely wiped out.

Thankfully, unlike the rats and that rooster, we humans and our friendly little prairie voles have pair-bonds, and pair-bonding species (after an initial mating frenzy) rely heavily on companionship, flirty behaviour (between partners), regular sex and affectionate touch to stay bonded and feel rewarded. Not on novelty. The novelty might still tempt us, but the fuzzy, warm feelings of a pair-bond can help keep us committed.

Cultured prude: Lovely. How lovely of...

Info dude: Wait up, Sir Culture. There is a but, there always is, a but.

But, too much competing stimulation (excessive sexual novelty) can hijack our reward circuitry and override the pair-bonding mechanism.

When scientists injected a prairie vole with amphetamines, a drug that stimulates the brain by releasing large amounts of dopamine into it our trusted, little mammal went all Tiger Woods on female voles. He did not pair-bond with anyone.[64]

You know what might be the perfect competing stimulation for a human brain?

Cultured prude: Hey wait, I know this. Something that stimulates our reward system and superstimulates it, internet porn?

Info dude: Yes, yes, Sir Culture. Research in humans also suggests that too much stimulation weakens pair-bonds. Even exposure to photographs of the opposite sex has a short-term detrimental impact on the pair-bond.

In a study, 87 men and 66 women participants were shown photographs of either attractive, underwear models (of the opposite sex) or photographs of abstract art.

After seeing the photographs, the participants were asked to rate their current partners on different attributes, such as physical attractiveness, intelligence, warmth, desirability and so on.

The results (obtained through mathematical computer analysis) showed that nearly always the men who had seen sexy, underwear models rated their partners lower than the ones who has seen abstract art.[65]

(Women were unaffected by photographs: more on that in the chapter 'Women on Porn'.)

Cultured prude: God, only photographs? What does that superstimulating internet porn do then?

Info dude: Eeeeexactly.

In the 1980s, when porn was still scarce, a study was conducted where a group of male and female participants were either shown videos of common, non-violent pornography or some non-pornographic content. Exposure was in hourly sessions during six consecutive weeks.

At the end of the six weeks, the participants who had seen porn reported a decrease in satisfaction with their intimate partners, especially with their affection, physical appearance and sexual performances. In addition, the participants assigned increased importance to sex without emotional involvement. There was no difference in the effects across gender and populations.[66]

Dozens and dozens of such studies show a direct correlation between pornography use and the weakening of pair-bonds.

In a study done with 20,000 adults who were married or had been in the past, it was found that adults who had seen a pornographic video in the past year were more likely to be divorced, have an extramarital affair, and were also less likely to be happy with their marriage.[67]

A study in the Philippines revealed that internet pornography consumption has an adverse effect on the relationship commitment of married Filipino couples. Furthermore, watching porn online weakened the relationship commitment that leads to an unstable relationship.[68]

A one-of-a-kind study spanning six years was done to check if frequent pornography use influences marital quality later on. In general, married persons who more frequently viewed pornography in 2006 reported significantly lower levels of marital quality in 2012. The frequency of pornography use in 2006 was the second strongest predictor of marital quality in 2012.[69]

A study done on adult women in the U.S. found a positive association between internet pornography viewing and more positive extramarital sex attitudes.[70]

(Yes, women can experience a breakdown of pair-bonds similar to men. More on that in the chapter 'Women on Porn'.)

Confirmed sceptic: You make porn sound terrible.

Info dude: I only give facts, Sir. (Wondering how many hours of porn viewing does not impact pair-bonds at all? Go to 'Good Porn'.) Now obviously some people do need to have a better sex life, there is nothing wrong with wanting more from your partner. What can be harmful is, to base that want on the fantasy that is today's internet porn, to let porn impact your intimate relationship without even realising it, to let porn erode our very delicate pair-bonds.

But since you insist, it looks like watching porn with your partner might actually be better than watching it alone.

> *One study investigated associations between viewing pornography and relationship functioning in a random sample of 1,291 unmarried individuals in romantic relationships. Individuals who never viewed porn reported higher relationship quality on all indexes than those who viewed it alone. Those who viewed it only with their partners though, reported more dedication and higher sexual satisfaction than those who viewed porn alone. The difference between the ones who never viewed porn and the ones who viewed it only with their partners was that the ones who never did, showed lower rates of infidelity.*[71]

From overstimulating our brains, to playing the part of sex education, to undermining our delicate pair-bonds, there are many more aspects to how today's internet porn is affecting our relationships, although a lot more research and studying is needed. Let the doctor speak:

Dr speak (*Manish Jain, Psychiatrist, Delhi*): I have had a couple where the husband could not perform sexually with his wife because he kept comparing her to the porn actors and he did not find her attractive because of that. I also have patients who have very little intimacy and intercourse with their partner. And they do indulge in a lot of porn viewing.

Dr speak (*Manoj Kumar, Psychiatrist, Technology Addiction, Bangalore*): There definitely is an impact of viewing pornography on intimate relationships. Some cases that have come to us show a significant decrease in sexual contact when too much porn is seen. Due to too much masturbation and exposure to sexual content, they don't feel as much need for intimacy or sex. Excessive use also leads to a decrease in communication between couples. There is usually a decrease in interest from one of the partners.

In a case study we did at our institute pertaining to pornography use in relationships, people demonstrated their concern about infidelity due to their partner's indulgence in accessing pornography. There was also the presence of psychiatric distress in the other partner.

Dr speak (*Sharmila Majumdar, Sexologist, Hyderabad*): Absolutely, there is an impact of pornography on relationships.

See, for a long-term, monogamous relationship, the values that exist in pornography clash so obviously with family concepts, that you know the potential undermining of traditional values of family, marriage and children. Pornography dwells only on sexual engagement with parties who have just met and are in no way attached to each other and will quite possibly never meet again. Sexual gratification in pornography is not a function of emotional attachment, of kindness, caring and respect. So obviously it has an impact on the family value concept.

Couples have come to me where the husband says 'Why can't I watch pornography?' or 'What's wrong with having another partner?'. These ideas have been set into them by viewing porn.

Also unrealistic expectations like their spouse should be of a particular dimension, should behave like this, do like that, indulge in some specific kinds of acts, which might or might not be acceptable to the partner, are set.

So, definitely it has an impact on long-term and marital relationships.

Info dude: Shit! It seems to get a little messy when today's dynamic, intimate relationships mix with super stimulating internet porn. Should a couple watch porn, should they only watch it together or should they never tell each other about watching it? Well, there are plenty of fun, non-overstimulating ways for couples to add spice to their relationships (more on that in the chapter 'Good Porn'). For now, let's move on to why both human and monkey brains love a...surprise!

And what that has to do with you deleting your porn history.

8

Surprise! (The Search for a Harder Hit)

It begins:

It was a beautiful evening, a Saturday night, one of those evenings that begs to be spent with friends. Rahul, Sid and I got together at Rahul's terrace. Whiskey, beer, food, music, the works. Things were primed for a night of pointless banter and a whole lot of stomach-hurting laughter.

'*Oye* Sid, you remember when this fucker got caught reading *Mastram* inside his Physics textbook by his dad?' Rahul never failed to bring up embarrassing stories.

'Ooo shit man, you remember that? It was the worst day of my life man, he slapped the hell out of me, and then he even took away my *Mastram*,' I recalled.

'Ha ha ha, why waste a *Mastram*, his dad must have thought!' Sid managed to comment between his laughter.

'Who the hell reads *Mastram* anyway? You were always a sick fuck, Amit!' Rahul added.

The stronger hit:

We settled in, the second round of drinks was made while we snacked on kebabs and nachos. Our discussion spilt in all directions.

'You guys are still smooth with women *yaar*. I have always struggled,' Sid said while stuffing his mouth.

'Well, not smooth enough man, I've always wanted to date two women at once, never happened,' I said.

'I did once, but the dream is to be in bed with two women at the same time,' Rahul smiled.

'Oh hell ya, that's the dream!' I nodded.

'Yes, *that* is the dream,' Sid agreed. 'It's my favourite kind of porn, threesome. Doesn't get better than that *yaar*.'

'I don't know, man, I try not watching that stuff, it depresses me. I will never be fucking two extremely hot women at the same time; it's just extremely unlikely,' I said.

'Ha ha, well yeah, or hot twins. But then you won't even get to fuck three dudes at once; you watch that shit,' Rahul said as he and Sid burst out laughing.

'Fuck you, dude! You know what, now that you bring it up, there is some seriously sick stuff on that hard drive you have given me,' I told Rahul.

'*Oye* fucker, you never disclose what you see in your friend's porn stash, that's the porn privacy code.'

Having known each other for quite a few years now, we did know a lot about one another, and on an evening like this, no topic was out of bounds.

Make that one stronger, will you:

'*Oye,* pour me a stronger peg; fuck, these kebabs were good,' Rahul said while chewing on the last piece.

'I think I'm drunk,' Sid announced.

'You get drunk like a chick, fucker. I heard you started dating, so you finally banging or what?' Rahul asked him.

'Oh no, no, not yet, we did do some second base stuff though. I am taking it easy *yaar*; I don't want to mess this up, I desperately need to get laid. I'm done jerking off.'

'Well, you're never done jerking off, man. I am having sex, I still jerk off. Like your three-way porn, now you will always want to jerk off to that.' I carefully poured myself another drink; I could already feel a lightheaded buzz.

'What's your favourite type of porn?' Sid asked.

'Yeah other than three dudes doing you, what else?' Rahul needled me.

'Fuck you! I don't know, man, it keeps changing I suppose. I do like some sick, hardcore stuff. Like bondage and shit.'

'I like bondage too. There is just so much new stuff out there now; you can go as sick as you want. What sick stuff do you like fucker?' Sid poked Rahul with his beer bottle as he said that.

'I like everything; I can watch any kind of porn, anytime. The filthier, the better. Ha ha ha,' Rahul replied.

We both nodded. It was funny how that statement sounded wrong, yet true.

Now that we're drunk, might as well get sloshed:

'Shit, it's over man, the fucking alcohol is fucking goooooone,' I cried. I was clearly drunk.

'Fuck *yaar*, Rahul, get some more *yaar*. We need more alcohol. We need more, more, we need it!' Sid was drunk.

'Fuckers, I can't walk down the stairs, I can't even fucking stand,' Rahul stood up, wobbled and sat down. 'See!'

'Fucking fuck *yaar*!' Sid lit a cigarette. 'I have to confess, guys. You two are my brothers, I have to confess. I fucking watch some very sick stuff these days. I watch shit that makes me feel sick, and I still watch it. I am a sick fuck,' Sid confessed in a drunken slur.

'What, even you Sid? I thought only this fucker likes watching POV* of being fucked by boys,' Rahul said and burst out laughing. He was rolling on the floor now. We all laughed for a bit, a self-perpetuating laughter.

'Fuck you, Rahul, straight *yaar*, straight, but sick. Like hardcore, punishment, rape, stepsister, fucked-up shit *yaar*,' Sid had just confessed to shit that you just never confess to. Unless you are drunk with your trusted friends, you never ever do.

'I watch that stuff too, man. I thought I'm the only sick fuck who gets hard on it,' I said.

Rahul smiled. 'Oh boy, stepsister *han*? I watch sick shit too, fuckers, so doooooon't worrrrry. We all do. Honestly, I do watch some real sick shit. I mean for some reason I have started liking some of that shemale stuff, it's so twisted, but somehow arousing, sexy. You guys know what I mean, right?'

> *Tolerance: The noun tolerance stems from the Latin for 'endurance'. If you build up a tolerance, you can handle large amounts of something (tolerate a large dose), without being too strongly affected.—Vocabulary.com*[72]

---

* POV: Point of View videos used especially in describing a method of shooting a scene or film that expresses the attitude of the director or writer toward the material or of a character in a scene. In porn, it describes videos that specialise in first-person point of view.

'Surprise!'

The Science of Surprise and the Need for Harder Hardcore Porn

Info dude: Dopamine! Today, we are constantly bombarded by stimulants. From WhatsApp messages, to Facebook likes, to getting new Instagram followers, to a news alert, to short, entertaining videos on *YouTube*, to going shopping, to eating sugary food—all of it stimulates our reward centres, it spurts out dopamine.

The Brain: See, I never experienced much stimulation in the earlier days (the last 50,000 years that is). The purpose of me being stimulated by new and novel things was to enhance learning, to give humans a reason to explore new territories, invent new tools. This, being stimulated all day every day is a very recent phenomenon. It is literally like I am being bombarded by stimulation all day long.

According to a study of Australian consumers, social media usage is a dopamine goldmine. 'Every time we post, share, "like", comment or send an invitation online, we are creating an expectation,' according to the study. 'We feel a sense of belonging.'

Info dude: Today's technologies are built to keep us stimulated, man. Yes, pressing that 'like' button on Facebook releases dopamine, but we don't even need to go that far, even a social media alert, that 'ting' sound on your phone, or just something flashing on the screen of your phone, indicating a message or an alert, will give you a rush of dopamine, triggering an urge to go check it out, to see what it is (That explains why once we do hear that 'ting', it is almost impossible not to check!).

And when you share pictures of those activities that naturally gives you a dopamine kick—your workout, a dinner date, your holiday—you get a second shot of dopamine from the sharing and 'liking' aspect.[73] (Shit, and all this while I thought it was my hidden artist making me take those pictures!)

The Brain: So in this over-stimulated environment, in order to truly grab my attention, things need to kind of stand out. This is where superstimulants come in (remember?). But here is the thing—when these superstimulants start showing up a little too often as well, I have to take steps to calm things down.

In an experiment, a group of rats were offered unrestricted access to their dream foods like bacon, sausage, cheesecake, and pound cake. These rats, as you would guess, couldn't stop binging to the point of becoming obese.

What the researchers found was that the dopamine receptors in the rats' brain had decreased. Dopamine receptors, as the name suggests, are the receptors (receivers) that accept the dopamine being released. With their numbers dropping, the amount of dopamine the brain was receiving also dropped. This drove the rats to binge more, in an effort to release more dopamine.

Two weeks later, the scientists returned the rats to their normal diet of 'rat chow'. The rats who had become accustomed to the stimulating food, chose to starve for a time rather than eat what was till two weeks ago their go-to food.[74]

Info dude: Yup, a similar decrease in dopamine receptors has been found in humans who overeat (more on this in 'Craving and Addiction').

Confirmed sceptic: Alright, alright, what are you on about mate, why the hell are you talking about dopamine receptors?

Info dude: Why I blabber about dopamine receptors, Mr Sceptic, is because of 'tolerance'.

This protective mechanism of the brain to reduce the dopamine receptors in order to keep balance is the reason we develop 'tolerance'.

This is a well-known feature of drugs of abuse. People need progressively larger and larger doses because the brain reduces its number of receptors. The same principle applies to sugar and junk food. There is also evidence that excessive exposure to violent movies/video games can build a tolerance towards violence.[75] And, guess what else can we build tolerance to?

 # A group of volunteers were shown non-violent porn. Repeated display of the film resulted in a progressive decrease in sexual arousal, which was accompanied by a reduction in the extent the men felt absorbed by the porn. Replacing it with a new porn video increased the sexual arousal again (novelty effect).[76]

 # An (Max Planck Institute) fMRI study found that more use of porn resulted in less activation in the reward circuitry of the brain.

Lead author Simone Kühn said the following about her study:

'This could mean that regular consumption of pornography more or less wears out your reward system. We assume that subjects with a high porn consumption need increasing stimulation to receive the same amount of reward. That would fit perfectly with the hypothesis that their reward systems need growing stimulation.'[77]

Info dude: Internet pornography stimulates the same parts of the brain that drugs and junk food stimulate. In fact, it is the sexual stimulation pathways that drugs like cocaine or heroin hijack.[78] Interestingly, heroin addicts often claim that shooting up 'feels like an orgasm'. Supporting their experience, ejaculation mimics the effects of heroin addiction on the same reward circuit nerve cells.

So once the brain becomes tolerant to a stimulus, a higher dose is needed to feel the same amount of pleasure. The higher dose for porn can come in the form of (the list that makes internet porn a superstimulant) more novelty, more stimulating camera work (HD, 3D porn), bigger and more enhanced body parts, or it can come in the form of shock/surprise.

Expert speak (*Tina Luna, Author*)[79]: Surprise hijacks all of our mental processes, everything we are doing and thinking. It stops it, pulls our focus into this one thing that surprised us, which is no easy feat in today's day and age when we are constantly distracted. Something else happens; our emotions intensify by about 400 percent when we are surprised. That's why if you get something as a gift that you weren't expecting, it is so much better than buying that same thing yourself. That's why when you want to delight someone with flowers, you don't call them and say, 'Hi, I am going to send you flowers at 2:35 pm'.

Info dude: Surprise, by definition, feeds off our love for the unexpected. Surprise gives us a boost of dopamine, as few other things can.

Scientist speak (*Robert Sapolsky, Neuroscientist*)[80]: We trained monkeys to press a lever for a reward. If they pressed the lever ten times, they would get a treat. As you can guess, every time they pressed the tenth time, their dopamine went up in anticipation of the reward. But this is where it starts getting interesting.

In a second variation of this experiment, the monkeys received the reward only 50 percent of the time. So they would press the lever and there was a 50 percent chance that they would get it or not get it, and they would be 'surprised' every time they got the reward. What happened to the dopamine? Dopamine shot up, twice as much of it was released in comparison to the last experiment.

In a third variation, the reward was given either 25 percent or 75 percent of the time. Surprisingly, the dopamine release for both 25 percent and 75 percent was the same, even though the monkey got rewarded more in the 25 percent, since the predictability was the same as the 75 percent. With 25 percent, the monkey mostly didn't get a reward. With 75 percent of the time, the monkey mostly got a reward.

When getting the treat was the most unpredictable (50/50), the amount of dopamine released was the highest.

Confirmed sceptic: Fascinating. Is this true for humans though?

Researchers at the Emory University 'split study participants into two groups. One group received a squirt of fruit juice into their mouths at predictable intervals, while the other group received juice shots randomly. MRI scans revealed that the group that received the juice at unpredictable moments, experienced more stimulation in the brain' (more dopamine).[81]

Info dude: When it comes to porn, we get that element of surprise every time we watch something which violates our expectations. We feel surprised every time we see porn that is more intense, more hardcore, and when we see newer genres. The following study demonstrates perfectly how tolerance impacts porn viewers and how quickly it can start being a factor in what kind of porn we seek out.

 # In this one study, common, non-violent pornography was shown to a group of male and female volunteers during six consecutive weeks. Another group was shown non-pornographic content for the same period.

After the six weeks were over, they were asked to come back two weeks later. On their return, both the groups were left in a private setting and given an option to watch different variety of videos (non-pornographic, common non-violent porn and uncommon, hardcore porn).

Male subjects who had seen the common, non-violent pornography showed little interest in watching the same again. Instead, they almost exclusively elected to watch uncommon porn (bondage, sadomasochism, bestiality).

This consumption pattern was far less pronounced in women.[82]

(More about how internet porn impacts women in 'Women on Porn'.)

 # In one of the first studies where porn viewers were asked directly about escalating porn tastes, 49 percent of the men interviewed reported searching for sexual content that they had previously found uninteresting and downright disgusting.[83]

The Brain: The earlier in my development this excessive sexual stimulation hits, the more tolerant I become of it, and the more extreme a stimulation I would need.

Results of a study suggested that deviant pornography (abnormal porn, i.e. incest, child porn, rape porn etc.) use followed an escalating progression in that individuals who started viewing porn at an earlier age were more likely to watch deviant porn compared to those who started watching at an older age.[84]

(More about the effects of pornography on a young mind in 'Kids on Porn'.)

The Brain: I can experience the stimulation of surprise in many different forms—novelty, shock, forbidden content, kink, seeking, etc. All these give me a much bigger burst of dopamine than the normal, one-on-one, vanilla sex video ever could.

A group of 18–34-year-old men were made to view either of the three different videotapes:

1) *An emotionally arousing videotape (depression-and-anger producing);*
2) *An emotionally arousing videotape (anxiety-and-anger producing);*
3) *A neutral videotape (a travelogue).*

Each of these was then followed by an erotic videotape. Sexual arousal was measured. Sexual arousal following the anxiety-and-anger videotape was greatest out of the three.[85]

Info dude: Depression and anger videotapes got the least amount of arousal; no one gets horny when someone dumps them, this we already know. But anxiety and anger work like a charm in getting us aroused this, most of us don't realise. So, in case you have ever wanted to—make out in a public space, done it in the car, got excited about make-up sex—now you know why. (Not all kinds of anxiety is good for arousal though—more on the kinds that is bad in 'Dysfunctional Dick'.)

A group of 21–30-year-old males who were trained to expect tolerance-level electric shocks viewed an erotic film under three conditions:

First condition: Volunteers viewed the erotic film in conjunction with a signal light indicating the threat of shock.

Second condition: A second light indicated the threat of shock if volunteers did not achieve an erection of a certain size.

Third condition: A third light indicated no shock.

The first and second (anxiety-inducing) shock-threat conditions increased penile size response over and above the no-shock-threat condition (third). Furthermore, the second condition with a more extreme threat had the maximum penile size response.[86] *(Wow, I know, shocking!)*

Info dude: No, no, don't start electrocuting yourself next time you can't get it up, that's not how this works!

One day you are watching an innocent video about a girl pleasing herself, next thing you are browsing through forced anal videos. That is what tolerance does, that is the nature of today's internet porn. It is completely natural to start seeking out extreme content.

A 2010 study had found that the majority of scenes from 50 of the top-rented pornography movies contained abuse, both verbal and physical, towards the female performers. Physical aggression, including smacking, open-hand slapping, and gagging, occurred in 88 percent of the scenes, while verbal aggression was found in half of the scenes.

The researchers concluded that 90 percent of the scenes contained at least one aggressive act where both physical and verbal aggression were combined.[87]

Dr speak (*Norman Doidge, MD, Author*)[88]: When pornographers boast that they are pushing the envelope by introducing new, harder themes, what they don't say is that they must, because their customers are building up a tolerance to the content.

Info dude: The demand for extreme porn is constantly pushing the porn industry into the realm of the more violent, the more shocking and the more surprising.

Pornstar speak (*Jules Jordan, Director and Actor, American Porn*): The thing about today's porn and the extreme market or the gonzo market, is that so many fans want to see so much more extreme stuff that I'm always trying to figure out ways to do something different...Fans are becoming a lot more demanding about wanting to see extreme stuff.

Expert speak (*Rashida Jones, Producer—Hot Girls Wanted*)[89]: Generally, if you're 18 and go to Miami, you're done in a year, because there's not enough amateur jobs for you. You can get some other jobs, but the niche stuff pays more, and the niche stuff is harder on your body.

Pornstar speak (*Lisa Ann, Pornstar*): Everyone's a ticking time bomb, and a lot of it is linked to the drugs that everyone is doing in the industry. A lot of this new pain comes from the new girls who have to do these abusive scenes because that does break you down as a woman.

Expert speak (*Rashida Jones, Producer—Hot Girls Wanted*): Then you have to make further negotiations with yourself, like, 'Will I do torture porn? Will I do fetish porn? Will I do [...] forced blowjobs?' and things that you never expected to do.

Pornstar speak (*Elizabeth Rollings, Pornstar*)[90]: I didn't want to feel the pain of penetration from an oversized penis or from being told to hold poses for still camera shots while being penetrated and choked. Every scene was at least two hours or more because of the need to do freeze-frame pictures and get good angles and lighting. I was degraded on camera and had to like it or else no pay! I was called names like bitch, whore, slut and because I was in the BBW (big, beautiful women) niche, my weight was consistently used as a form of exploitation and insult.

Pornstar speak (*Rachel Bernard, Pornstar*): I was scared. I didn't know that I could tell him no, or the fact that we had already recorded for 15 minutes that I could fucking leave…then what? Then I understood that that's how rape victims feel.

Confirmed sceptic: Man, that got very intense, very fast. Do you think women react to this internet porn any differently than men?

9

Women on Porn

'Do you girls ever talk about sex with each other? Like guys will not discuss details, especially if we are serious about the girl. I know if I tell my friends details, they will be imagining my girlfriend naked the next time they see her,' I asked my childhood friend Tanya. She was the only female friend I had; the only one I could call a good friend. You can't really have female friends when you have sexual fantasies about every decent looking girl you meet, the only kind of girls you can then genuinely be friends with are the ugly ones. Tanya wasn't ugly though, in fact she was quite pretty, but for whatever reason I did find it easy to be just good friends with her.

'Well, it depends, dude. With my close, female friends, I might discuss some stuff. It depends, it depends,' she replied while fiddling with her phone.

'Give me an example of the stuff you discuss with them. Do you talk about dick sizes and shit?' I probed further.

She looked at me with disgust. 'What? Don't be stupid. We don't talk about dick sizes. You've been watching too much *Sex and the City*. We talk about things. I know guys talk a lot about sex; if not about your own sex life, then what the hell do you talk about?'

'Well, we talk about porn a lot. Like we will discuss disturbing details about the disgusting kinds of porn we watch. By the way, I've never asked, do you watch porn?'

'Umm, not really. Like, I prefer reading it,' she said.

'Oh yeah? And what about your other friends? Do all of them prefer reading? Women just don't like watching porn, isn't it?'

She smiled and shook her head. 'You boys really don't have a clue about how women are sexually, do you? You meat-head!'

'Well, yeah, I'm a meat-head, now tell me.'

Tanya then went on to give me a fascinating insight into the female mind:

'I was doing a sleepover at Preety's house. You know Preety, my friend from school? It was her and Shikha; she is also an old friend.

Not sure how the conversation had started, but I told them how I find the whole *Redtube, Pornhub* type business disgusting. First, they both agreed with me, but then Shikha smiled and said, "Actually, I watch porn all the time, I love it. I'm not even sure why I said I don't. Just this stupid notion that women should not watch porn."

So, Preety and I both say that's cool, I mean there is obviously nothing wrong with women watching porn. But I honestly tried and it just didn't do it for me. Preety agreed. "My boyfriend has literally begged me to watch it with him. He thinks it's somehow very sexy to watch porn while having sex. But it just doesn't work for me."

Shikha then told us, "I watch a lot of bondage—BDSM stuff."

BDSM action and Shikha...who would have thought! She has always been this very introverted, sweet girl. But it turned out we were just getting warmed up. Preety then dropped her bomb, very casually. "I actually don't mind watching lesbian porn once in a while. Have I told you girls about this time I kissed a girl?"

So, she has full on smooched a girl at a party! I ask her the obvious question, "But you're straight, why the hell do you watch lesbian porn? Why did you kiss the girl? Jesus, Preety!"

"I just hate the normal porn that's out there, it is so aggressive. Lesbian porn is just more loving and sensual, you know what I mean? And I just randomly kissed that girl *yaar*, I was drunk."

And what else? Yeah, this one was interesting, Shikha has a favourite bondage porn actor and all. He apparently has a penis that can make a horse insecure! Preety, however, prefers medium-sized penises.'

'Wait, wait, wait! I thought you girls didn't discuss penis sizes?' I interrupted Tanya.

'Oh, shut up. This conversation is over. I've told you a lot more than I should have anyway. You keep your mouth shut.'

Tanya went back to her phone. I sat there, digesting all this new information about Shikha and Preety. 'But what about you, what kind of porn do you read?' I continued to pester Tanya.

'Oh come on, seriously? Are we still having this conversation?'

'Wha...? I'm just curious, dude. It just gives me more ammo to decode women. It's not sexual in any way, Tanya. I just want to know what turns women on,' I pleaded my case.

'Arrgh! Okay, well I read everything! Women get turned on equally by weird stuff. Stuff they probably will never want to do in real life. Also, mostly, it depends a lot on my mood. That's it! This topic is over!' she said with finality.

'What the hell is wrong with you? I had said we will watch some threesome action today, not actually do it!'

The Science behind It

A bunch of scientists measured men and women's genital response to different sexual images. Men mostly got aroused to either images of adult women or men; women, on the other hand, responded sexually to a much broader range of images. In fact, women had a (small) physiological response to images of bonobo chimps mating (yes chimpanzees, Discovery channel style). Moreover, women's physical response was often at odds with their verbal descriptions. In other words, what women said they found arousing did not always correspond to their actual physiological arousal.[91]

Info dude: In other words, female sexual arousal (some might claim female behaviour in general) is confusing, even to the women themselves.

In a research, when sexual images of the opposite sex were shown to both men and women, they found that compared to women, men showed greater activation in the left amygdala (deals with giving meaning to the world) and showed heightened arousal in the hypothalamus (deals with sexuality) and in the brain's emotional centres.

Basically, the male brain was just more excited about porn than the female brain. Hence, the researchers argued that men find sexual images more compelling than women do. Simple enough. But, when researchers asked study participants about how arousing the images were, the women, overall, rated them as more sexually arousing than men.[92] *(Bam! Deal with it.)*

Info dude: As I said, confusing, to everyone. (I can see some men nodding in agreement.)

Northwestern University researcher J. Michael Bailey and colleagues got participants in an experiment to view erotic videos and answer questions about their levels of sexual arousal, while the researchers actually measured their levels of arousal through devices attached to their genitals. (Don't start imagining what the devices look like. Focus!)

The participants included straight men and women, and gay men.

Now as you would expect, all was obvious and predictable in the land of men, both straight and gay. Straight men said they found the boy/girl and girl/girl action exciting, while the gay men found the boy/boy action exciting.

In both the cases, the measuring devices backed up their claims.

With the women though (yes, there is a pattern here), the results were surprising and revealing.

While the straight women said they found the boy/girl action exciting, their devices showed the same levels of excitement to boy/girl, girl/girl, and boy/boy action.[93]

Scientist speak (*J. Michael Bailey, Sex Researcher*): Women may be more open to same-sex relationships thanks to their less-directed sex drives. Women probably have the capacity to become sexually interested in and fall in love with their own sex more than men do.

Many studies support Dr Bailey's statement, sexuality most definitely seems to be a much more 'fluid' state among women than men.

Info dude: Yes, that's a better word—fluid. Female sexuality is more 'fluid' than male sexuality.

Remember Coolidge effect, the love for novelty that men have? Well, when it comes to women, the novelty effect seems to be a bit more, what's the word here, oh yes, fluid.

There are studies where female subjects have shown reduction of sexual arousal to repeated viewing of the same pornographic content and an increase in sexual arousal when a new novel video was shown.[94]

While in another such experiment only a slight decline in genital responding was observed. Women sustained considerable levels of genital arousal even after 21 trials of uniform pornography stimulation.[95]

Dr speak (*Ajay Nigalani, Neuropsychiatrist, Sexologist, Delhi*): Females need that emotional day-to-day connection that comes with an intimate relationship; males are less bothered about it. So what is expected out of an act is different for men and women.

From an evolutionary point of view, the male only gives his seed, but the female will have to carry a baby for nine months and then nurture the child for many years after that. So, what she is looking for in a partner is a lot different to what a male is looking for.

Info dude: One difference between the sexes seems to be originating from the all important hormone—testosterone. We know that testosterone plays a crucial role in the lives of human males. Some might even argue that testosterone has shaped human history. Although it is primarily known as a male hormone, testosterone is present in a much smaller quantity in women as well (ten times less than men).

Testosterone in men has been linked to many behavioural and physical traits. Sexual desire for one is deeply linked with testosterone levels, low levels of testosterone in our body can result in a loss of sexual desire, it can also lead to erectile dysfunction (ED). A long period of sexual inactivity can also result in a drop in testosterone levels.[96]

Testosterone has also shown to increase sex drive in women.[97]

In a very interesting case study, a woman called Griffin Hansberry who went through testosterone treatment in order to change her gender, experienced some fascinating changes in her sexual behaviour. Keep in mind that she was being injected with doses of testosterone which were higher than that found in a healthy male.

> *'My sex-drive went through the roof,' Hansberry says. 'I felt like I had to have sex once a day or I would die. I was into porn as a girl, but now (as a man with large amounts of testosterone) I'm really into porn.'*[98]

Dr speak (*Paras Shah, Sexologist, Ahmedabad*): It seems that men, due to high levels of testosterone think about sex more often than women do. Women have lower levels of testosterone, so they are not that obsessive about sex.

(* *This theory about testosterone is not backed by much research, and hence, it is only a possible theory.*)

Info dude: Another big difference in the way women see sex, seems to originate from the 'way' they see sex.

> *The same researchers who had found the male brain indulging in more activity while watching porn but women claiming to be equally or more aroused, did a follow-up study. They had study participants view hundreds of sexual photos from porn websites as their brains were being scanned and eye movements being tracked. They were also asked to rate the photographs on how arousing they found them. The researchers then analysed the data they collected: which images were found arousing by whom, exactly what parts of those images were the participants looking at, how was their brain reacting to all this, etc.*
>
> *Interestingly, as it so happens, men and women did look at different aspects of the images—and they rated different types of images as more or less arousing.*

Indo dude: So porn does turn women on, but when it comes to what exactly is turning them on, and how is it affecting them, the answers seem to be a lot more complex. For instance, cultural influences seem to have a significant impact on female sexuality.

Female sexual attitudes, practices, and desires are more influenced by their environment than men.

Research indicates that women are more likely to change their attitudes towards various sexual practices over time.

Interestingly, women who regularly attend church were more likely to have conservative attitudes towards sex, while no such correlation was found in men. (This is very relevant in our country where religious, cultural taboos have been dictating female sexuality for centuries.)

Women are more likely to base their decisions about sex on the sexual attitudes of their peer group.

Another very relevant study showed that women with a higher education were more likely to have experimented with different sexual practices (like oral sex); while education made less of a difference with men.

Women show more inconsistencies between their expressed values about sexual activities (like premarital sex, BDSM) and their actual behaviour around those activities.

Dr speak (*Sharmila Majumdar, Sexologist, Hyderabad*): First, in our country, there is absolutely no sex education. Men are given more freedom, they have more access, and they can go watch porn with friends or whatever else. Whereas women are treated more conservatively and therefore have fewer opportunities to watch it.

Secondly, women are nurturing by nature, hence even if they experimentally watch porn, they probably would like to stay off it. This is also because family values are drilled into them. So they do watch it, but the percentile is very less, compared to men.

Info dude: Although viewing pornography could be viewed as a sexually liberating experience for women, a gender which has been sexually repressed and controlled for centuries, some research suggests that today's internet porn (with its violent content) might be having exactly the opposite effect.

In one academic study, 304 random scenes were selected from different porn websites on the internet, and it was found that 90 percent of them showed some form of physical aggression against women like spanking, gagging and slapping. While at least half of all the scenes contained verbal aggression, against women.

These stats become particularly disturbing and scary when you start exploring the extent at which porn is influencing young women.

 # In a recent Swedish research it was discovered that, like young boys (more on this in the next chapter), young girls are now using pornography as their principal source of sex education. It discovered that 43 percent 16-year-olds fantasised about mimicking what they saw, while 39 percent had gone ahead and tried them.

 # And as many as 40 percent of girls between 13–17 years in England say they've felt pressured into a sexual activity.[99]

Info dude: Women and their higher susceptibility to be sexually influenced by the environment has been misused to manipulate female sexuality from centuries, the current hypersexualised culture is not exactly free of its own manipulative qualities.

 # In a fascinating study, it was measured if a woman's attitude towards a man's gaze would change, following exposure to explicit pictures of other women. The pictures were of varying degree of explicitness. It was found that women who were shown more explicit photographs (with lesser clothes on) expressed greater acceptance of the male gaze than women who were shown less explicit pictures. The reactions were studied immediately after the exposure and also at an eight-hour follow-up. The study shows how even brief exposure to explicit centrefolds can have an effect on women's sociosexual attitudes.[100]

 # Research is showing how women can experience many types of sexual insecurities and body image-related issues, all due to watching porn.[101]

Dr speak (*Angela Clifton, Sex and Relationship Psychotherapist, Nottingham University*): Often young women do stuff to please the guy. It's less about their enjoyment and more about guys saying: 'If you like me, you'll do these things.' In the long term, I think it will have (negative) emotional consequences.

Confirmed sceptic: So, just to be clear, if the porn is violent, degrading to women, and so on, then women seem to have a negative reaction to it. What about all other kinds of porn?

Info dude: Glad you brought that up, because it turns out there are ways in which pornography impacts women, in quite the same ways as it impacts men.

 # Male and female volunteers were either shown a pornographic video or a non-pornographic video in hourly sessions during six consecutive weeks.

The group that had consumed pornography reported less satisfaction with their intimate partners—specifically with their partners' affection, physical appearance, sexual curiosity, and sexual performance. On top of that, the volunteers who had seen porn assigned increased importance to sex without emotional involvement. These effects were uniform across gender.[102]

Info dude: Many more of such studies are showing how pornography consumption is informing our sexual scripts. These scripts acquired through porn are then used by many consumers (both men and women) to inform their sexual attitudes.[103]

Dr speak (*Ajay Nigalani, Neuropsychiatrist, Sexologist, Delhi*): Medically, a woman too should be affected by porn as much a man is being impacted.

Dr speak (*Aastha Sachdeva, Psychiatrist, Child Psychologist*): It should not affect them differently, but the effect it shows on them is probably different. For females, the signs of any sexuality-related problems are different to men.

Info dude: You know the whole mirror neuron and dopamine thing and how the superstimulant internet porn can use them to mess with a male brain? Well, women have the same reward mechanics. Although watching pornography might not always stimulate a woman's reward circuitry much, but if and when it does, then what follows is quite similar to the effects seen in men.

A study examined 51 female internet porn users and 51 female non-internet pornography users.

Results indicated that porn users rated pornographic pictures as more arousing and reported greater craving due to the pictures compared with the non-users. The porn users also displayed craving, greater sensitivity to sexual excitation, problematic sexual behaviour, and greater severity of psychological symptoms. Findings confirm the reinforcing nature of sexual arousal.[104] *(So, once a stimulant rewards the brain with dopamine, the brain wants more of it, irrespective of gender.)*

Info dude: Then there is the whole 'real sex versus porn' routine, which women are no less susceptible to.

A large sample of adults were surveyed during a research, two-thirds of which were women. A worrying trend was noticed by the researchers.

The research suggested:

A large number of women are feeling disappointed by real-life sex. Some reasons cited were: sex they see in porn lasts longer than what they are experiencing, they don't experience orgasms as easily as women do in porn (where all it takes is a touch), and the gargantuan penises in porn are hard to match in real life.

Watching porn is resulting in both men and women expecting increased performance from their partners, which is resulting in real-life sex seeming dissatisfactory.[105]

Dr speak (*Paras Shah, Sexologist, Ahmedabad*): I have had many female clients who come and say their partner's penis size is small as compared to the penis they see in porn. Also, they complain about their partner not doing it multiple times in a day, like they see in porn. They say their partner does it once and then forgets about it for a few days.

They also come with anxieties about their breast size as they are worried their partner likes big breasts.

Dr speak (*Ajay Nigalani, Neuropsychiatrist, Sexologist, Delhi*): Day before yesterday, a guy came to me and said he was in a new relationship and his girlfriend said he has a small penis. My question was where is your girlfriend getting that idea from? Well, she got it from porn.

Women across the world are opening up to doctors and on various online forums on the internet, about how porn is impacting their life. A regular porn user in one of the online forums reported how constant exposure to internet porn has started to make her feel highly sexed.

'I had lost my virginity to a boyfriend before university, but after I started watching a lot more porn, it was all about hook-up sex and one-night stands. Sex became like starring in my own porn film in my mind, and I thought I knew exactly what to do.'

However, what she had found liberating at first soon started to feel 'soulless' to her. The men she was with, loved that she was ready for anything and everything they too had seen in porn.

'I realised that here I was, an educated, young woman, volunteering to behave for free like pornstars who were paid, or forced, to pretend they were enjoying it.'

Info dude: Again it is important to point out that female sexuality has been repressed and subverted for centuries, and hence a woman breaking free from cultural taboos and expressing her sexuality in whatever way she wants can only be a good thing. But research is suggesting that many women might be jumping from one form of subversion to another kind. To allow the porn industry, which is driven primarily by profit, to define what female sexuality should be like, seems to be hindering the true liberation of female sexuality, rather than enabling it.

There is obviously nothing wrong with wanting more from a sexual partner either, what is important is to not base that want on the fantasy that is internet porn.

Women are different to men, especially when it comes to their sexuality. In a large survey, about 40 percent of women reported some sort of sexual problem—most commonly low sexual desire—but only 12 percent said they felt distressed about it. A lot of factors go into the delicate mix that triggers desire in women. Clearly, more research is needed for a better understanding of things.

Talking of female sexuality, you know what is the one thing which is not ambiguous at all? The impact of internet porn on kids!

10

Kids on Porn

What does the new generation think about life, about sex and about porn? Here's a glimpse:

Isha (*19 years old, lives in Delhi, First-year Architecture student*): Hi guys, I am Isha, and a student of Architecture. The course is full on, I mean I still have four years to go before I become an architect. It feels like I will be dying of old age by the time I finish. But that's okay, because I do kind of enjoy it. I have made some amazing friends this last year. I have even started dating someone! It's not a big deal, but I do like him a lot. Like a lot, lot. He plays in a band, and he is handsome, and he has the sexiest smile ever (smiles).

My parents live in Nagpur, so I live in a PG accommodation here in Delhi. I go back to Nagpur whenever I can, but I don't really get much time to. Also, the gang from college always ends up making plans when we have an extended weekend or something. It has been life-changing, moving to Delhi, all by myself. Like I never even entered the kitchen at home, now I have to make my own meals and shit. Also, I always thought clothes got washed magically, I left them lying around in my room, and somehow, a day later they turned up all clean and ironed. Hah! I know, I was a bit stupid.

Yes, of course, I've seen porn. Well, honestly, I only saw it for the first time last year, here in Delhi. My friends at the PG decided to get drunk one night and watch porn. It was some guy giving this girl a massage. And honestly, my first reaction was 'yuck', I was grossed out. Especially with the ending, the guy actually ejaculated on the girl's face, it was disgusting. I told my boyfriend about it, and he laughed it off, saying I'm being stupid, everyone does it these days. God, everyone does it? I don't understand, it doesn't seem sexy at all. But I guess I have a lot to learn about sex. I have since managed to watch it a few times without getting grossed out. But I prefer porn with some sort of storyline to it.

Rohit (*16 years old, lives in Bhopal, father is a doctor, mother a housewife*):

Yes, I am Rohit. Hobbies, hmm—I play football in school, like hanging out with friends, and I love gaming. It's more than just a hobby though, gaming. I mostly play WOW, World of Warcraft. I am actually the best WOW player in my school.

Oh yes, I do have a girlfriend. I have more than one actually. But Naina is the one I like the most. We have gone second base, and third base is coming soon, hopefully. My parents are going away next weekend; I'll probably have her over and hopefully will score third base (chuckles). The maid will be home, but you know, I can deal with her quite easily.

How to have sex? Of course, I know how to do it! Ha, are you kidding? We do have internet in Bhopal you know. Most of my friends have already done it, and they have told me all about it too. But you can't really trust the guys with such information, you never know how much of what they say is bullshit.

But yes, I have seen enough sex on my computer to know what I need to know. With the POV videos, you feel like you're actually doing it. Although Naina might not know much about it, as I am her first boyfriend. But I can teach her, that's not a problem.

Ritu (*14 years old, lives in Ahmedabad, father is a civil engineer and mother a teacher*):

Hi. I have just entered ninth standard. I love to draw and write poems. I scored 82 percent in eighth standard and ranked third in class.

My mother is a little strict. She is always telling me how if I don't come first, I will have no future. My father is not strict at all; he does whatever I tell him. He just gets worried about me sometimes.

Oh no! Of course not, they can never know! They don't know that I have a boyfriend. I don't think my father will approve and Mom will definitely kill me if she found out. She will just lose it if she found out that I bunked school with him last week. Yes, it was my first time. I was terrified, I was so terrified. But it was fun, I had taken a change of clothes and we went and saw a movie. I like him a lot, he is handsome. He is my senior and all the girls in my class are jealous that I'm dating him.

Porn? Mmmm, yes, I have, but it's not like I watch it often or anything, in fact, I hardly ever watch it. And yes, my parents can never know about this too. They won't understand how it is. You see most of my friends in school have phones or tablets. One day, a friend had sneaked a phone in her bag, and we watched porn in school on her phone. It was strange; I didn't even see all of it. I also saw it with my boyfriend after that. He has a phone too, and he showed it to me. It was weird; I don't know, it was very strange. My heartbeat goes through the roof when I see it. I think I did like one of the videos he showed me. My boyfriend watches a lot of porn. I guess everyone does.

Divik (*12 years old, lives in Bangalore, both parents work in IT companies*):

Hi, I am Divik. I don't like school; actually, I hate it. The bag is just too heavy, and the teachers are all boring. Except for my English teacher...she is great. She even made me act in a school play recently. I am very good at acting; I am also my school's junior football team captain. My favourite actor is Robert Downy Jr, and my favourite football player is Neymar.

Yes, we do have girls in our class, it's a co-educational school. All the girls are annoying though. Except for this one girl who I like a lot, she has very long hair. She likes me too; she keeps looking at me and smiling. I have tried kissing a girl once—she was my neighbour, we were playing, and we tried kissing. I didn't like it at all.

Yes, I have seen dirty videos. All my friends have. When my friends come over to my house to study or play video games, we usually end up watching some scenes from a movie, or we just Google sexy videos and explore the websites that come up. I have my own laptop, so it's quite safe; I always remember to delete the browsing history. I have one friend who actually watches full-on porn, every day; he has also shown porn to some girls in my class, he is crazy. What if my parents found out? Well, I know they watch it too. I checked my dad's browser history one day, and he for sure watches porn.

[Adolescence: The developmental years. From when puberty hits to 18–19 years of age, possibly more.

Puberty: Between 9–16 years old, could be more or less. Varies greatly with each kid.]

'I don't care if all your friends at school have a subscription of hornymilfs.com. You are not getting one.'

The Science behind It

Cultured prude: *Aah,* now our Indian kids, they are much more cultured than these Westerners, you cannot deny that, dude.

Info dude: You, Sir Culture, make statements and use words in those statements that make no real sense. Our kids, especially in urban India, are living in a reality which is vastly different than any of the previous generations ever grew up in. In fact, one can argue, that the generation gap between modern Indian kids and their parents is much starker than the generation gap in any of the western countries. And none of this has anything to do with 'culture', the world is simply different now, especially the world our kids are growing up in, and that is just how it is. It is a world full of gadgets, videos games, and a world where kids are constantly connected to everyone around the planet through the internet.

According to a survey, most urban Indian kids in the age group of 9–17 are spending multiple hours a day on the internet, mostly through mobile phones.

It estimated that 134 million Indian children are connected to the internet already, and these numbers are bound to keep rising. The survey also estimated that 95 percent of urban Indian kids from nine years and above are accessing the internet from various devices today, and 62.4 percent of them spend up to four hours a day online.[106]

Confirmed sceptic: Okay, they have internet access, we all do. So what?

Info dude: Well, internet access is great, but kids you see, are different from adults, especially when it comes to being curious about things.

Dr speak (*Aastha Sachdeva, Psychiatrist, Child Psychologist*): During adolescence, the exploration and curiosity levels are very high.

Info dude: You already know this. Kids' curiosity is what makes them fun and annoying at the same time. A combination of curiosity, and all those hormones that follow puberty (testosterone in men and oestrogen in women), and kids tend to become overly interested in one particular subject matter. Mr Brain, please carry on.

The Brain: A prime evolutionary task of an adolescent me a.k.a. brain is to learn all about sex—both consciously and subconsciously. So if anything anywhere promises to tell me more about this most fascinating subject, on which the survival of human species depends, I jump on the opportunity.

Dr speak (*Dr Sanjiv Kumra, MD, MBBS*)[107]: Adolescence is a time where the most important function is really to prepare you for mating. All the brain changes that take place during this time are happening to prepare the organism to be able to carry out that central and important function.

Confirmed sceptic: Curiosity + puberty + internet access = Oh, I see where you're going.

> *A recent study indicated that the timing of puberty and the start of sensation-seeking behaviour predicted the use of internet pornography. Boys that were in an advanced stage of puberty, more frequently used internet pornography.*[108]

Info dude: So yes, our kids are watching internet porn, they are biologically compelled to, and they are watching it at an increasingly younger age.

Over 50 percent of porn users in India are under 24 years old.[109] That doesn't sound terrible. Well, some reports say that the average age a kid sees pornography today is at 11 years old.[110] This is the 'average', mind you, not the youngest.

Dr speak (*Aastha Sachdeva, Psychiatrist, Child Psychologist*): I have come across kids as young as 11 years old watching porn. And these are the ones who got noticed. They may not say it directly, but you can infer from their behaviour and after some digging they tell you they are watching porn.

Dr speak (*Manoj Kumar, Psychiatrist, Technology Addiction, Bangalore*): Through a research done in Bangalore, we found that with the adolescent group in the research, the majority had seen pornography, mostly because of curiosity or due to peer pressure.

Info dude: The reality is, that a kid doesn't even need to be looking for explicit content and is still likely to stumble upon it sooner rather than later. A child growing up in urban India (increasingly in rural India as well) is going to look at porn at some point. It's inevitable.

Confirmed sceptic: Oh, yes I guess they will. Well, I guess we already know about how it will impact their brain then.

Info dude: Oh no, no, no, Mr Sceptic, how pornography impacts an adolescent brain is a whole lot different. You see an adolescent's brain works differently:

1) An adolescent brain gets much more excited about things. It releases more dopamine than an adult brain.

 # Scientists made electrode recordings to get data on how neurons in the brain react to a reward. The same reward was given to both an adolescent rat and an adult rat. Upon receiving the reward, the adolescent brains lit up with excitement to much higher levels than the adults, in the brain region that weighs reward and punishment.[111]

 # Neuroscientists at the University of California 'scanned the brains of 19 adults (age 25 to 30) and 22 teenagers (age 13 to 17), while the participants played a gambling game. During the games, the participants had to decide

whether to accept or reject a bet with a 50-50 chance of winning or losing various amounts of money'.

In the brain scans, the Reward circuitry of the teenagers' brains lit up more than in the adults' brains.[112]

Effect on viewing pornography:

Info dude: By now we know how dopamine makes us want things. Well, adolescents experience a stronger rush of dopamine, and thus a more intense wanting towards whatever resulted in the dopamine release (in our case, pornography). In response to novelty provided by internet porn, an adolescent's brain produces higher spikes of dopamine.

2) The adolescent brain is still not fully developed.

Info dude: A growing number of recent neuroimaging researches have demonstrated that during adolescence and till much later after that, the brain is still growing and changing.

Dr speak (*Sandra Aamodt, PhD, Neuroscientist*)[113]: Brain scans show clearly that the brain is not fully finished developing until about the age of 25.

The process of changes that starts around puberty, is only about halfway through by 18.

Info dude: So, what parts of the brain are still growing till the twenties and what effects do they have on behaviour?

Dr speak (*Sandra Aamodt, PhD, Neuroscientist*): It's the prefrontal cortex, which is not yet fully developed till the twenties.

Info dude: 'Prefrontal cortex' is a part of the brain that is situated right behind the forehead. This part of the brain takes the longest to develop, and it is home to brain functions such as planning and impulse control (the ability to control one's impulses). These functions may not get fully developed till the mid to late twenties (I know, I know, suddenly a loooot of things start making sense!).

A study done with people of different racial and ethical backgrounds, living in five different countries, found that while reasoning powers do mature early in humans, impulse control, the ability to think of future consequences to behaviour and resisting peer pressure slowly develop well into the twenties.

Effect on viewing pornography:

Dr speak (*Manoj Kumar, Psychiatrist, Technology Addiction, Bangalore*): The prefrontal cortex part of the brain, the reasoning part of the brain of an adolescent is still developing, they are not able to reason out properly about what will be the consequences of watching porn. But their emotional part is developed and hence they are able to enjoy the activity. So, there is more tendency to explore.

3) An adolescent brain struggles to plan for the future.

One of the consequences of delayed prefrontal cortex development is the hindered ability to plan for the future.

The capacity to plan for the future in different age groups was examined in individuals between 10 and 30 years old. The younger half of the group showed a consistently weaker orientation to the future. They were willing to accept smaller rewards delivered sooner rather than bigger rewards that were delayed. They also consistently characterised themselves as less concerned about the future, and less likely to be able to gauge the consequences of their decisions.[114]

Effect on viewing pornography:

Info dude: The ability for delayed gratification is very low in adolescents (i.e. the ability to put off something mildly fun or pleasurable now, in order to gain something that is more fun, pleasurable, or rewarding later). If they encounter something like porn which provides them instant gratification, they are much more likely to ignore any long-term consequences and go all out on a binge.

4) An adolescent brain is much more susceptible to peer pressure.

Dr speak (*Sandra Aamodt, PhD, Neuroscientist*): The prefrontal cortex is the part of the brain that helps you to inhibit impulses and to plan and organise your behaviour to reach a goal. It acts as a filter that helps us gauge which impulses are good and which are bad. One of the side effects of these changes is that adolescents and young adults become much more sensitive to peer pressure than they were earlier or will be as adults.

So, for instance, a 20-year-old is 50 percent more likely to do something risky if two friends are watching than if he's alone.

Researchers did a simulated driving study and found that when teens did the simulation by themselves, they drove as well as the adults. But when those same teens were told to take the same driving simulation with two friends in the room, the number of chances they took doubled! The presence of friends, however, made no difference to the driving of adults.

Effect on viewing pornography:

Dr speak (*Manish Jain, Psychiatrist, Delhi*): I have been dealing with kids who have been introduced to pornography by their peer group. I have had a case where the kid was being shown porn by his seniors.

Info dude: Almost all Indian doctors agree that most kids are first shown pornography by the peer group and when all their friends are watching porn, you can be sure that our susceptible-to-peer-pressure adolescent will watch it too.

Confirmed sceptic: Hmmm, our human kids are a bloody mess.

Info dude. Well, we are not the only animals with impulsive adolescents:

Many animals like the gazelle (antelope), otters, parrots, elephants, all suffer from delinquent adolescents.

> *Adolescent sea otters are known to swim into dangerous waters, risking being eaten by sharks. Adolescent gazelles are known to approach and follow predators, instead of fleeing. Adolescent parrots are known to exhibit behaviours like bouts of being prone to biting, yelling, and sometimes masturbating on their owners (hah!).*[115]

Cultured prude: But I don't understand, why do these kids have to behave in such an uncultured way?

Info dude: These adolescent behavioural changes in humans and in other social mammals, although they may lead to danger, exist for a reason; they are as natural as natural behaviours come. They give the adolescent an evolutionary advantage by encouraging separation from the comfort and safety of the family.

The behaviour changes also foster the development and acquisition of independent survival skills.

The only problem is that we humans live in a starkly different world now, and just like the super-stimulus of internet porn or junk food can hijack our ancient brain's needs, similarly, today's porn can tap into the evolutionary changes that come along with adolescence.

5) An adolescent brain can easily lose track of reality.

Dr speak (*Manoj Kumar, Psychiatrist, Technology Addiction, Bangalore*): Immersion phenomena: I have seen it a lot in video game users, where the player gets so lost in the game that they lose all touch with the real world.

Dr speak (*Aastha Sachdeva, Psychiatrist, Child Psychologist*): Kids start associating this online material which is putting them into a fantasy world with their real world. It is called 'social realism' where adolescents start associating fantasy with the real world.

Effect on viewing pornography:

Dr speak (*Aastha Sachdeva, Psychiatrist, Child Psychologist*): The utility factor for a pornographic video is very high according to an adolescent's brain. Because they feel whatever they are watching online, it is stimulating enough and they feel it will be useful in real-life experiences. So, they can start abusing the content because they feel it is useful to them.

6) An adolescent brain is primed to form long-lasting associations and habits.

Info dude: Okay, so first, let's understand how habits are formed:

Dr speak (*Deann Ware, PhD, Neuroscientist*)[116]: Our brain cells communicate with one another via a chemical transmission. One brain cell releases a chemical (neuro-transmitter) that the next brain cell absorbs. When brain cells communicate frequently, the connection between them strengthens. Messages that travel the same pathway in the brain over and over, begin to transmit faster and faster. With enough repetition, they become automatic. That's why we practice things like hitting a cricket ball. With enough practice, we can go on autopilot.

Info dude: And, this process of forming habits and patterns in the brain (going on autopilot), happens much more easily and faster in an adolescent brain (The reason why we find it easier to learn new sports or languages as a kid). The brain actually shrinks after age 12 as billions of nerve connections are pruned and reorganised.

Synthetic Pruning

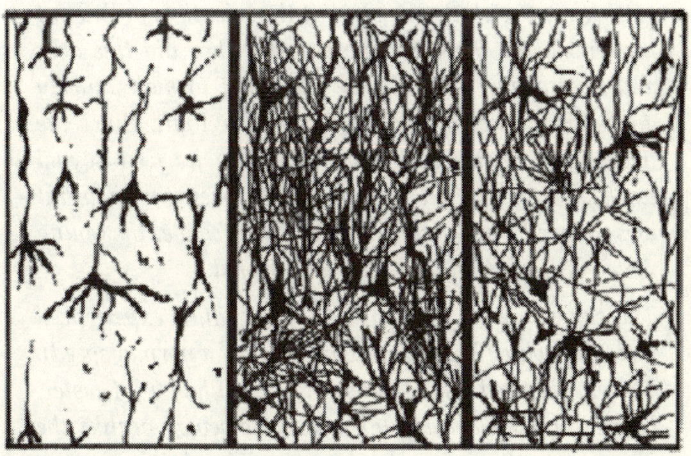

at a child's birth | at 7 years of age | at 15 years of age

The use-it-or-lose-it principle governs which nerve connections in the brain survive this pruning process. Once these new connections form, the brain holds on tightly to these associations.

Research shows that the most powerful and lasting memories and habits arise from adolescence.

Effect on viewing pornography:

Info dude: All this pruning and habit formations and stuff—what it really means is this—an adolescent's brain wires together experiences and arousal much faster and more easily. An adolescent brain quickly forms long-lasting habits around whatever sexual activity it sees or engages in.

What better way to understand sexual conditioning in kids than to peek into the lives of some horny virgin rats, right?

> *Scientists introduced a receptive, female rat in a cage with a virgin, male rat, and as expected, the virgin rat started getting sexy with the female, but the scientists pulled out the female rat after just one minute. They did this over and over again, till the male rat learnt to mate quickly and started ejaculating within the time limit. Since the male had learnt this behaviour during its first sexual experience, it stuck with him. Even when the male rat was allowed uninterrupted access to a female, the young male ejaculated a lot faster than normal.*
>
> *The same process was tried with an adult, experienced male rat (which had learnt to have sex at a normal speed). The experienced male too learnt to ejaculate a lot faster, before the female was pulled out. However—unlike the young rat whose sexual behaviour did not change even*

after the conditions changed—the older rat when allowed to have uninterrupted sex again, went back to the normal mating behaviour.[117]

Info dude: How far can we push this sexual conditioning thing? Apparently, till death.

Researcher Jim Pfaus placed sexually receptive females inside a cage with virgin, male rats. But Jim made a slight change, he had sprayed the female rats with a substance called Cadaverine (has an odour of decaying flesh). Now, normally rats have an innate hatred of Cadaverine-type smells, they will avoid the odour of decay at any cost.

But since this was a chance for the young males to lose that damned virginity, with their dopamine soaring in adolescent anticipation, they went ahead and mated several times with the females. (You can't beat that dopamine urge, and as we know, there is greater amount of dopamine release in adolescents.)

Here is where things started to get really interesting though. When a few days later the researchers put those rats inside a cage with two groups of females, one smelling like death and the other smelling like how a normal receptive, female rat should smell like, the Cadaverine-conditioned rats got it on with the deathly smelling females and ignored the other group. Normal, experienced males refused to go anywhere near the females that stank of death.

Info dude: Can we push it even further? Apparently yes, till the point of changing sexual orientation. Yes, you read that right.

Researchers placed a male rat with another male rat. They injected one of the males with dopamine three times in eight days (thus imitating in him the buzz of sexual arousal).

A few days later, the male who had been conditioned to feel sexually aroused around another male was placed in another cage with his male buddy and a sexually receptive female. What do you think happened?

His behaviour indicated that he was much more interested in the male rat than the female. He did not turn 'gay', as in, he did not mount the male rat, but his sexual behaviour had definitely veered towards same-sex attraction.

Confirmed sceptic: Wow, but surely this does not mean watching pornography can change a human kid's sexual tastes, no way.

Info dude: Mr Sceptic, you keep underestimating the powers of internet porn.

In a study, the age of first exposure to internet porn was found to be significantly correlated with frequent and addictive internet porn use. The study subjects with earlier exposure to internet porn were more likely to have longer porn sessions, use porn more frequently, and were more likely to score higher on Internet Pornography Addiction Criteria.[118]

Info dude: Research after research is showing how using internet porn at a young age has far-reaching consequences on a kid's sexual life.

 # Results from a research done in 2013 have suggested that, individuals who start watching adult porn at a younger age were more likely to watch deviant pornography (bestiality porn, child porn, incest porn, etc.) compared to those who start watching it at a later age.[119]

 # Another, more recent research from 2016 indicated that people that watch deviant pornography and had scored significantly high on openness to experience those acts, were more likely to have started seeing porn at a younger age compared to adult-only pornography users.[120]

Info dude: It seems clear that human beings' early sexual experiences are critical in forming their sexual characteristics, their habits, their tastes, and their likes/ dislikes around sexuality. And, increasingly they are being formed through watching internet porn.

Teens around the world are already beginning to realise that watching internet porn is having unwanted consequences. A poll done in 2014 with 18 year olds across the UK found the following: 67 percent agree that pornography can be addictive; 70 percent agree that porn can have a damaging impact on young people's views of sex or relationships; 66 percent agree that porn is pressuring girls or young women to act a certain way; 72 percent agree pornography leads to unrealistic attitudes towards sex.[121]

Info dude: It is important to remind everyone that we are talking specifically about internet porn, the superstimulant, and not random nude pictures in a magazine. And there is no ambiguity as to if internet porn, with its superstimulants, is harmful or not for adolescents—it is harmful! To know more about how then do we deal with the reality where they are almost guaranteed to watch it sooner rather than later, go to 'Advice for Parents'.

Let's move on to the most curious effect porn is having on men, and their erections.

11
The Dysfunctional Dick

One year, one whole year. Twelve months, actually twelve months, two weeks and five days, so twelve and a half months, more than a year, god damn! I didn't even remember what sex felt like. Sure I had been wanking my ass off all this time, but shit I wanted the real thing. Out of nowhere, she had landed in my life, like Batgirl, or Wonder Woman, my saviour. As if sensing my desperation, she had wasted no time in agreeing to come spend some sexy time in my apartment.

The date was fixed, preparations were made and the list of things I would do to her memorised. I had been preparing for this day for a year now, more than a year. My taste in porn had matured during this time, porn itself had matured. In spite of government attempts to ban some porn websites, the sites and the variety they offered just kept exploding. India as a country was embracing porn, with its own cartoon, porn series *Savita Bhabhi* becoming more popular than Shah Rukh Khan and the very sexy, former pornstar Sunny Leone being accepted as a mainstream actress. There were all these moves and tricks that I had been dying to do on a real girl and this was it, the day was here and I was already exploding with anticipation.

She was stunning, the best piece of ass I ever had a chance to have sex with, not only that, she was experienced, and she demonstrated that experience right off the bat. Removing my pants she got to work, oh boy, she knew what she was doing. I could not hold it. No worries though, we waited for a bit and she got to work again and we were right back at it. The fun had now begun. I did all those porn moves, going down on her like a pro, she loved it, things were on track. I got that condom on, to begin some real action, but the bloody wrapper would not come off, by the time I managed to tear it with my mouth and get it out, my thing was not hard enough to get it on. Bummer. Not to worry though, she saw what the problem was and got to work, and soon it was hard as a rock. I quickly got it on this time, and we were having sex. It was wonderful, amazing, exhilarating, so we decided to change positions, doggy style, hell yeah. But as I moved behind her, my rock had softened, and I knew that the position would not work. It didn't make any sense; I had never ever in my life had a problem with not being hard enough, never. She was so hot, and I was having so much fun, but my dick seemed to have other plans. WTF! She finally suggested we let it be for now. Cursing my penis and with a resolve to make her beg me to stop the next time around, I let it go. The next time came soon enough. This time I didn't masturbate for a few days before the all-important day, you know, just to make sure I am feeling it throughout. She looked hotter, she did her thing again, and soon I was hard as a rock again. The condom did come on right away, it was all looking good, till we did the changing position thing again, and again, the fucker went limp; I wasn't giving up this time, so I closed my eyes and imagined my favourite porn scenario, played a scene in my head and bam the boy was hard, so I got it going. Worked for ten seconds and then limp again. I tried it again, and again, and again, till the point it got too frustrating and I just jerked off in front of her; somehow that worked. Another day another try, three is a charm, this time while I was inside her and she was getting ready to orgasm, my dick just went. Fuck it, I'm done, limp attack. Needless to say the girl with all that experience looked at me with pitying eyes, and moved on to better, stiffer things. Bummer.

> *'Even the world's greatest actor cannot fake an erection.'*
>
> *—Unknown*

'It's not you, it's me.'

The Science behind It

Confirmed sceptic: Hold on, hold on now, you are not about to suggest that pornography causes erectile dysfunction, are you?

Info dude: Alright, I'm holding on, and for once, Mr Sceptic, your scepticism seems legitimate. Firstly, let's establish what erectile dysfunction (ED) is. It isn't the lack of interest in sex, or not being turned on by your partner. When I say erectile dysfunction, I mean the inability to either have an erection, keep an erection, premature ejaculation, or the inability to ejaculate at all, when the person is turned on and desires to have sex. Any of these erection problems in men are also called erectile dysfunctions (ED).

Dr speak (*Ajay Nigalani, Neuropsychiatrist, Sexologist*): For a male to participate in a sexual activity, he needs an erection. So with ED either you have a problem getting an erection or sustaining an erection—that is erectile dysfunction.

Info dude: Now, erectile dysfunction is a medical condition, and anyone suffering from it, should first consider seeing a doctor.

Confirmed sceptic: Hmm, but why are we talking about this quite inappropriate topic, *han*? Anyway, this ED thing seems to be a rare medical condition or something.

> *According to a study published in 2015, it is estimated that 320 million men in India could be dealing with erectile dysfunction.*[122]
>
> *'One out of every ten Indian males could be impotent, according to a survey of 1,500 men done in Delhi.'*
>
> *A recent, seven-year study by the Marital and Psycho-sexual Clinic, Chandigarh, concluded that 77 percent of its 464 new patients suffered from ED or premature ejaculation or both.*[123]

Dr speak (*D. Narayana Reddy, Sexual Medicine Consultant, Chennai*): I now see at least 15 patients a day (for ED-related problems); back in 1982, I had just 37 patients for the whole year.

Dr speak (*Ajit Avasthi, Psychiatrist*): What we are diagnosing is not even the tip of the iceberg.

Confirmed sceptic: Jesus, alright so this ED is quite common, but what's your point?

Info dude: Pay attention, now these between-the-legs disappointments are of two kinds—physical and psychological.

Dr speak (*Ajay Nigalani, Neuropsychiatrist, Sexologist*): There is a physical aspect to ED—hypertension, diabetes, medications, lack of hormones, alcohol, smoking, etc.

Then there is a lot to do with the psyche.

Info dude: And it turns out that psychological reasons are quite often to blame for these erectile problems.

Dr speak (*Rupin Shah, Director, Centre for Male Reproductive and Sexual Medicine, Mumbai*): Almost two-thirds of all cases of impotence in India stem from psychological causes.

The brain plays a key role in triggering the series of physical events that cause an erection. A number of things can cause or worsen erectile dysfunction like depression, anxiety, stress, relationship problems, and other concerns.

Info dude: While ED was always a problem mostly faced by older men, there is a growing trend of young people experiencing erectile issues:

> *According to a 2013 study in the* Journal of Sexual Medicine, *nearly one out of four new erectile dysfunction (ED) patients is under the age of 40.*
>
> *This is a surprising finding, given that ED has always been an affliction of men in their sixties and seventies.*[124]
>
> *Traditionally, ED rates among young men were always around 2 percent, in the last few years though, data from around the world is indicating that this percentage has jumped up to 14–30 percent, even 50 percent in some cases.*[125]

Confirmed sceptic: Damn, why is that though? What has changed in the last few years? Oh wait, no, is it?

Info dude: Well, there could be many reasons for this sharp increase (stress, unhealthy lifestyle, etc.), but one of those reasons, I am afraid seems to be internet porn!

So much so that a doctor from the Harvard Medical School has even coined a word for it: porn-induced erectile dysfunction!

In one of the first studies that got porn viewers to answer directly questions about their escalating porn tastes, the results showed that higher sexual desire, lower overall sexual satisfaction, and lower erectile function (ED) were associated with problematic porn viewing.[126]

A Belgian study has also found problematic internet porn use was associated with reduced erectile function and reduced overall sexual satisfaction.[127]

Info dude: This next one leaves little room for doubting if pornography can impact the libido.

The experimenters got a group of young men (average age 29) to watch pornography. While they were doing this to check their arousal response, what they were not expecting was the results that they saw—50 percent of the young men did not get any erections with porn.

The shocked researchers then allowed the men to choose their own liking of porn (more hardcore/kinky action) and the no-erections rate dropped down to half. The men in the research group acknowledged that they had high exposure to hardcore porn, which was probably why they were having trouble getting it up with normal porn or getting it up at all.[128]

Info dude: These libido bummers are becoming so common in young men that the most unlikely of places are seeing cases of ED, caused by guess what?

In an extensive review, US Navy doctors provide the latest data revealing a tremendous rise in youthful sexual problems in the US Navy. The doctors include clinical reports of servicemen who developed porn-induced sexual dysfunctions.

The first, a 20-year-old, active duty serviceman described how he has not been able to reach an orgasm with his fiancée from the past six months. He could achieve an erection but could not orgasm. His erection too had become a lot more short-lived than before he started having ED issues.

The serviceman reported that he had started masturbating frequently 'years ago' since the time he had gained access to internet pornography. He relied solely on internet porn for masturbation. Initially, he would watch soft-core porn and that was enough, but he gradually needed more hardcore, graphic, more fetish-driven porn to orgasm. He would watch multiple videos simultaneously, watching the most stimulating parts of those videos.

The second, a 40-year-old African-American serviceman reported not being able to maintain an erection during intercourse with his wife.

He reported that six months ago their youngest child had left for college and since then he had found himself having a lot more privacy; which led to him watching porn and masturbating a lot more often. First, he would masturbate once a week, which increased to 3–4 times a week. His taste in porn started with soft porn, but soon he was not able to orgasm with that which led to him using more graphic material (Explained in the chapter 'Surprise!'). Soon thereafter, sex with his wife was 'not as stimulating' as before and at times he found his wife 'not as attractive'.

He reported never having these issues earlier in their marriage.[129]

Info dude: Doctors from across India are reporting plenty of similar stories, where men are unable to perform in the bedroom and a regular dose of pornography consumption seems to be a running trend in most of those cases (See the chapter 'Porny Relationships'.)

Confirmed sceptic: But wait. How can porn, which turns people on (causes an erection), ever cause a decrease in erections? This doesn't make any sense.

Info dude: Yes, yes, Mr Sceptic, your scepticism is yet again legitimate, but here is the thing. You remember our dear, old friend dopamine?

You see, to have an erection, one needs a constant supply of dopamine: Studies have found that central dopamine is a key neurotransmitter in the control of sexual function. A steady stream of dopamine is imperative in sustaining an erection.[130]

Info dude: So our good, old dopamine works in odd ways. We know the following: it shoots up when something is better, more novel, than what we expected (surprise), but dopamine also drops to below normal when the expectations are not met.[131] With real-life sex, it is almost impossible to match the novelty, variety, surprise (the supernormal qualities) of internet porn. So, when a man accustoms himself to porn, real sex may not meet his subconscious expectations. Which will result in a drop in dopamine levels, and hence a drop in erections.

Dr speak (*Shwetank Bansal, Neuropsychiatrist, Sexologist, Delhi*): I have had couples come to me where the wife is dismayed by the fact that the husband prefers masturbating to porn than having sex with her. He is finding real sex unfulfilling, because the expectations are different.

For example, take domination or bondage where people tie each other up for sexual excitation. Of course, that is completely consent based. Now, if someone has been watching a lot of that in porn and wants to try it in real life, but the partner is not okay with it, that will lead to a conflict, because that person needs it to be aroused. So there is a dopamine drop that will happen, and real sex will not arouse them. Therefore, it is not really upto a pornography viewer after a certain level to regulate what they want to do and not want to do. Because once they are in, the dopamine gets them hooked. They watch a harder, more intense version of porn to get a dopamine high, and then when real sex cannot match that high, it leads to lower levels of dopamine and hence decrease in libido.

Dr speak (*Sharmila Majumdar, Sexologist, Hyderabad*): If someone is watching a lot of porn, there might be situations where they are not able to perform with their wife or partner.

The reason being unfulfilled expectations—they want their wives to act like that, behave like that, do all those kinds of things, that they see in porn, which may or may not be acceptable to the partner.

The Brain: Well yes, there is the unmet expectations, and there is the fact that my reward circuitry, where dopamine does all the work, actually gets worn out when someone regularly watches internet porn, resulting in less dopamine in the reward circuitry (hence resulting in lack of arousal with normal sex or vanilla porn). This process is also called desensitisation (a lot like tolerance) (more on that in the next chapter).

Info dude: You see, with internet porn, that dopamine rush is just too god damn easily available.

Dr speak (*Shwetank Bansal, Neuropsychiatrist, Sexologist*): With real-life sexual contact, dopamine levels rise to standard predictable levels. But with pornography it can quickly escalate into higher and higher doses of dopamine, and also it is like a switch. You can click and press the switch and get a bigger rush of dopamine at any time. So you keep pressing the switch over and over and over again. However, real life pales in comparison with that, because there is no switch in reality. Real life is a lot more complex than that.

I have had couples come to me where the wife is dismayed by the fact that the husband prefers masturbating to porn than having sex with her. It is because he is getting a bigger dose of dopamine from porn.

> *A 2017 study found that the more pornography the participants of the study watched, the more likely they were to prefer porn over a human for sexual excitement.*[132]

Info dude: More dopamine not only makes it harder to 'get hard' when the dopamine is not as abundant, it also trains the brain, it conditions it.

Dr speak (*Norman Doidge MD, Psychiatrist, Psychoanalyst, Author – The Brain That Changes Itself* and *The Brain's Way of Healing*): Pornography seems to be a purely instinctive matter: sexually explicit pictures trigger instinctual responses, which are the product of millions of years of evolution. But if that were true, pornography would be unchanging. But, the content of pornography is a dynamic phenomenon which illustrates the progress of an acquired taste.

Info dude: Acquired taste—like that time as a kid when you had alcohol for the first time and hated it; look at you now, you proud tequila shots guzzling, fine wine drinking you. You acquired the taste of alcohol. Studies have shown that sexual arousal is conditionable in both men and women, and especially so in kids. How we humans get aroused, what arouses us, is not 'set' in stone. It is fluid. We can 'acquire' sexual tastes.

See, the nerve cells that fire together, wire together. In other words, the brain makes connections, that is how it works. For instance, when something sexually excites us a lot, the brain makes a connection between sexual arousal and the memory of the events associated with the excitement. For example, type in your favourite porn site and you activate nerve cells that blast your reward circuitry. Up goes your dopamine.

Much as Pavlov's dog learned to salivate† (get hungry) to the bell, today an internet porn user wires together unexpected/unwanted signals to his arousal.

And it turns out, men can train their arousal to the point of erection failure.

Dr speak (*Harry Fisch, Urologist, MD*): A penis that has grown accustomed to a particular kind of sensation

---

† Russian psychologist Pavlov rang a bell every time he gave his dogs food; soon the dogs were trained to start salivating every time the bell rang, in anticipation of the food. https://www.simplypsychology.org/pavlov.html

leading to rapid ejaculation will not work the same way when it's aroused differently. Orgasm is delayed or doesn't happen at all.

Info dude: There is also the element of anxiety (the kinds that kill libido) that can follow the unrealistic expectations that are perpetuated by today's pornography.

Dr speak (*Shwetank Bansal, Neuropsychiatrist, Sexologist*): A lot of young adults are getting exposed to pornography for many years before they have actual sex. So when the time comes to have real sex, there can be a lot of misconceptions and anxieties that can cause ED. They are expecting themselves to perform for one hour and so on. When you are anxious about your performance, erection won't happen.

With medicines like Viagra, 90 percent of its use is for recreational purposes, where people who are not medically required to have it use it. So they are just taking it to meet the expectations which they think their partners have, without even discussing it with them. They think that the girl expects that one should last this much and have a penis size that is this much. This all mostly comes from viewing pornography.

Info dude: Not everyone who is watching porn simply stops getting an erection. It works in much more subtle ways. Put simply, sexual conditioning, sensitisation, or other sexual arousal-related brain changes occur on a spectrum. Also, realise that our brain is constantly learning and adapting to the environment. Internet porn, being a supernormal stimulus targeting innate sexual circuits, shapes the brain, alters perception, and eventually impacts a man's ability to get an erection.

Confirmed sceptic: Damn! But with a dozen different reasons for why someone might be having ED, how can anyone tell if it's due to porn?

Info dude: Great question! You, Mr Sceptic, can be useful once in a while.

Expert speak (*Gary Wilson, Physiology Teacher, Author*): Now, to know if a guy's sluggish sexual performance is related to porn, they should try this:

1) See a good urologist and rule out any medical abnormality.
2) Next, on one occasion, masturbate to your favourite porn.
3) Then, on another occasion, masturbate with no porn and without fantasising about porn. Compare the quality of your erections and the time it took to climax (if you can climax). A healthy, young man should have no trouble attaining a full erection and masturbating to orgasm without porn or porn fantasy.

If you have a strong erection in (2), but erectile dysfunction in (3), then you probably have porn-induced ED. If (3) is strong and solid, but you have trouble with a real partner, then you probably have anxiety-related ED. If you have problems during both (2) and (3), you may have progressive porn-induced ED or a below-the-belt problem for both of which you should get medical help.

Confirmed sceptic: Hmmm, this is all very interesting, but I still am sceptical that a man will ever choose porn over an actual woman.

One of Playboy Mansion's official playboy bunny, Hugh Hefner's official ex-girlfriend, Izabella St James, in her

> *book* Bunny Tales *writes about having sex with the most famous playboy in the world, Hugh Hefner.*
>
> *She described how Hefner would have sex twice a week, with four or more of his extremely hot-looking girlfriends, St James being one of them. He had everything a man could dream of, the novelty of the hottest looking women who were willing to do anything that he pleased. At the end though, writes St James, came the 'Grand finale: he masturbated while watching porn'.*
>
> *So a man, who was living the ultimate porn fantasy, with actual pornstars, chose to watch people having sex on a screen over the real thing.*[133]

Info dude: Now, that should settle it, Mr Sceptic, really!

In the next chapter, I tell you tales of more celebrities behaving like our *Playboy* king Hugh Hefner. Internet porn is impacting us in subtle ways, the full scope of which we don't even understand yet, clearly more research and studies are needed. But a decline in the control over one's erection (in varying degrees) is evidently one of those subtle ways in which internet porn is impacting men.

Did things get a little too intense for you with all that talk of flaccid penises? Okay then, just to make things more entertaining, let's dive into the penultimate chapter about pornography's impact on our minds. We all know heroin is addictive, we have seen it in the movies, we have all felt the power of junk food when we stood in front of a delicious-looking cake and felt a tangible craving to eat it. The obvious question then is, can pornography be addictive? Can it cause cravings? What the hell is addiction anyway?

12

Hooked on Porn

'Dude, did you hear that? Tiger Woods! Man, he was doing it with like a million different chicks. Addicted to sex they are saying, also addicted to porn. God damn!'

'It's so stupid, man, sex addiction, do you believe in that shit?'

'They actually have sex addiction clinics, rehab centres. Amazing!'

'Like, who isn't a sex addict? I think about it all the time, but what I need is more sex, not rehab, ha ha ha!'

'Dude, this porn addiction is a real thing in the US. So stupid, man!'

'Fucking first-world problems, dude. They live such privileged lives, they have to look for problems that don't exist.'

As I was returning from hanging out with my friends, I couldn't help but smirk at the thought of porn addiction. I had never heard that before, sex addiction I could still understand, it was stupid, but I could still imagine it being a thing. Like if I had hundred naked women in front of me, I would probably keep doing it till I die of dehydration or something. I would definitely need help then. But porn addiction just seemed ridiculous. One of those ideas that some conservative, religious freak would come up with. I got back home, had a bath, ate dinner, and retreated to my room. It was 11.30 pm, I had to get up at 7 am the next day. I better sleep, I thought. But I had already switched on my laptop, so I decided to do a quick Facebook check, and then call it a day.

Oh two birthdays, let me check who (click). Harmeet, who the hell is this? Divik, oh my school friend who I haven't met in four years, his brother Divik, whatever (scroll down). A random statement about politics and the ensuing heated discussion (scroll down). Oh this friend's friend is in Italy; wow, pretty place, he looks happy, lucky fuck (scroll down). Some music video, it's too damn late for a music video (scroll down). Random shit (scroll down). Ah, my cousin from Mumbai, she and her friends, nice (scroll) oh wait, who is this girl with her. Damn, she's kind of hot. I should go meet my cousin in Mumbai sometime; nice friends, wonder what this one's name is (scroll down a little) maybe she has commented on it, or liked it, she must have. Ooh there she is, 'Roma Trivedi—lots of love kisses'. Ooh Roma, what a fucking hot name, let's have a look (click). Twenty-two, doing an MBA, here we go, photos (click). Oh man she is fine (scroll, click, scroll, click). I could marry this chick right this fucking moment, look at that ass, dear lord, has there ever been a better-looking ass, ever. Let me just quickly shag. Need to see more though, let me find a porn girl who looks like her, fuck yeah (Google—Porn—Indian with a hot ass). Ooh boy, hell yeah, now we're talking. This one, yes, that ass (click). Alright, alright, let me just browse around while this buffers (scroll down to similar videos). Ooh this one, let's just (right click, open in a different window), and this one (right click, open in a different window), dear god this one looks (right click, open in a different window), oh man this one....

Just then my phone rang, I was pulled back to the real world, fuck it was 12.30 am. One of the friends I was hanging out in the evening with was calling.

'Yo,' I answered. 'What? Dude, it's past midnight, I don't care what you're doing right now, I'm going to sleep. Come on, man, why are you telling me if you're watching porn, go fucking watch...No you're not, I was watching porn too, what's wrong with that, everyone watches it...Well, then don't watch for a while and you will know if you're addicted or not...No, I won't try not watching as well, I fucking love porn and I will keep watching it, now fuck off, I need to wake up early tomorrow.' I hang up. What a fucking loser I thought, thinks he is addicted to porn, after all that discussion we had. Anyway, I need to get up early, so let me just quickly shag and sleep (click). Ooh man the videos are ready to play! Bring them on. Let me just watch this one (click) and I will be done. (After ten minutes) Let me quickly have a look at one last ass, and then I can...(click). Okay, this one is the last and then I'll just...(click).

'I now pronounce you, addiction and addict.'

The Science behind It

Info dude: *Aah* addiction, that fuzzy feeling you get when you can't stop thinking about someone. 'I'm addicted to you,' you tell her/him.

Addiction, that craving you can't ignore, when you just have to get a bite of that chocolate/cake/pizza/whatever. 'Oh I'm addicted to chocolate,' you chuckle with your friends.

Addiction, that euphoric feeling that follows a run/gym session/that game. 'Man, I'm addicted to running, feels like shit on days that I don't.'

Addiction, that urge to smoke a cigarette. 'I must smoke after eating, it just seems like the perfect thing to do after a meal.'

Addiction, that thing you know some people suffer from, perhaps someone in your family. 'Oh that poor guy, he ruined his life because of his addiction.'

So, what the hell is addiction?

> *Addiction is a condition that results when a person ingests a substance like alcohol, cocaine, nicotine (substance addiction) or engages in an activity/behaviour like shopping, gambling, sex (behavioural addiction) that can be pleasurable but the continuation of which becomes compulsive and interferes with ordinary responsibilities and concerns, such as work, relationships, or health.*[134]

Info dude: The heroin junkies, the alcoholics, the smokers, they are all 'substance addicts'. We know this addiction, we recognise it. But behavioural addiction can be harder to spot and recognise. Can internet porn then be a type of behavioural addiction?

Dr speak (*Sharmila Majumdar, Sexologist, Hyderabad*): There are three A's to any addiction. Accessibility, affordability and availability. These three are all applicable to pornography these days.

Confirmed sceptic: No, no, I have never seen anyone go to porn rehab, surely porn can never be addictive addictive.

Info dude: Yes, Mr Sceptic, I have never seen anyone go to smoking rehab either (Do they even exist?), but we all know smoking is addictive addictive. Addiction, Mr Sceptic, is a broad spectrum. Addiction to different behaviours or substances shows up in different ways. But research shows that at the root, they are all quite similar. They impact the same parts of the brain.[135]

For example, rats that are addicted to a substance can easily switch between sugar, amphetamine and cocaine.[136] (Proves how they are primarily working on the same parts of the brain.)

Info dude: Internet porn is no different, it impacts the brain in much the same ways as most other addictive behaviours or substances do.

A Cambridge University study found the same brain activity pattern in porn addicts (users with excessive porn use) as seen in drug addicts and alcoholics. The researchers also reported that 60 percent of subjects (average age: 25) had difficulty achieving erections/ arousal with real partners, yet could achieve erections with porn.[137] (Supporting the finding in the chapter 'The Dysfunctional Dick'.)

Dr speak (*Manoj Kumar, Psychiatrist, Technology Addiction, Bangalore*): In our own research and case studies we are seeing the similarities between porn addiction with substance addiction. We have a case study where a boy was abusing cannabis then alcohol and then he came back to cannabis. He then started viewing pornography; once he started excessive use of pornography his cannabis use came down. This is indirect evidence that porn replaced his cannabis/ alcohol addiction and hence is working on the same parts of the brain.

Info dude: Internet addiction is now accepted as the mainstream addiction, there are tons of studies proving a link between internet addiction and other forms of addictions. If internet use itself is addictive, then obviously internet porn use is too.

A research was done to check the addictive powers of various activities which can lead to compulsive internet use. The research was conducted within an interval of one year. In the end it was found that the participants who indicated they spent a lot of time on watching pornographic content were most likely to be spending more time in compulsive internet use one year later. Amongst all the internet applications, erotic content seemed to have the highest potential for becoming addictive.[138]

Info dude: What makes pornography addictive in the first place? How does it affect the user in ways which could potentially make it addictive?

1) Hypofrontality, turning adults into adolescents:

Info dude: Remember, how an adolescent brain is not fully developed, especially the prefrontal cortex part, the decision-making part of the brain (from the chapter 'Kids on Porn')? Well, it turns out excessive exposure to internet porn (or any kind of drug) can make an adult's prefrontal cortex behave like an adolescent's.

 # In a study conducted in 2015:

Participants completed a pornography use questionnaire and a delayed gratification task; they were then asked to take the same questionnaire and task four weeks later. Participants who had reported that they watch pornography more, demonstrated a lower ability for delayed gratification. The participants who abstained from pornography use, demonstrated higher ability to delay gratification, four weeks later.[139]

 # A latest study in 2017 showed how exposure to sexual stimuli induces reduced self control.

The researchers noted that: porn use increases impulsivity and may reduce certain executive functions (self-control, judgment, foreseeing consequences, impulse control).[140] *(Which is really not that shocking a finding, is it? Most of us have experienced sexual arousal interfering with our decision-making powers.)*

Dr speak (*Aastha Sachdeva, Psychiatrist, Child Psychologist*): Addiction or over-consumption of any material can have major cognitive consequences. All higher-order thinking skills, whether it is reasoning, problem solving, decision making, motivational abilities or concentration abilities, are all getting impacted with any kind of addiction.

Dr speak (*Manoj Kumar, Psychiatrist, Technology Addiction, Bangalore*): We did a small, sample-size study where we found there is some evidence that excessive users of gaming/porn find it very difficult to control their response, and they find it very difficult to switch to offline activity. This phenomenon is also found in substance abuse, suggesting that there are similarities in how substance addiction and technology addiction impact the brain. We have found this in other experiments as well.

2) Desensitisation: The characteristics of needing a bigger hit.

Info dude: We know how porn can build tolerance (See the chapter 'Surprise!'). Excessive stimulation of the reward circuitry results in the reduction of dopamine receptors in the brain, resulting in the need for a bigger burst of dopamine to experience the same amount of stimulation.

Obesity has these characteristics too. Obese people need a bigger hit of dopamine (more sugar-rich, fatty food) to feel the same amount of pleasure a non-obese person might get from a healthy meal.[141]

Similar decrease in dopamine receptors has been seen in porn users (details in the chapter 'Surprise!').

Just like there is a tendency for porn users to escalate to more extreme versions of porn, desensitisation can also lead to addictive pornography viewing.

Dr speak (*Shwetank Bansal, Neuropsychiatrist, Sexologist, Delhi*): What is built into the addictive behaviour is tolerance. You need increased amounts of pornography—in terms of duration or in terms of intensity (in terms of the kinds of porn you are watching). A lot like it is with alcohol or other drugs.

Dr speak (*Sharmila Majumdar, Sexologist, Hyderabad*): Once you start watching pornography, it is not as simple as deciding that you just don't want to watch it anymore. It becomes a pattern, it gets conditioned. Maybe in the first 3–5 months of watching porn, you may still be able to control it easily, but eventually it will become a habit-forming activity.

Any addictive activity stimulates the reward circuitry. Whether it is gambling, or alcohol, or pornography. And once something rewards your brain, you will want to go back to it again and again.

The need for harder and harder genres of pornography in order to reach the same level of stimulation; the struggle to get erect with real women—these are all part of the desensitisation process.

3) Novelty. That guaranteed burst of dopamine.

Info dude: To pay attention to novelty has been critical for human survival. The release of dopamine due to novelty is what drove us to explore new environments. Super stimulants use this very preference for novelty that our brain has, to hijack our behaviour (see the chapter 'Dopamine, the Drug of Desire').

Expert speak (*Gary Wilson, Physiology Teacher, Author*): Internet porn is especially enticing to the reward circuitry because novelty is always just a click away. It could be a novel 'mate', unusual scene, strange sexual act, or—you fill in the blank. And the most popular porn sites have built this pursuit of novelty into their layout. Every page presents dozens and dozens of different clips and genres to choose from. They are engrossing precisely because they offer what seems like inexhaustible novelty.

Dr speak (*Sherry Pagoto, PhD, University of Massachusetts*)[142]: Studies on appetite show that variety (novelty) is strongly associated with overconsumption. You will eat more at a buffet than you will when a sandwich is the only thing on the table. In neither scenario will you leave hungry but in one you will leave regretful. In other words, [if you want to negate overconsumption and its problems] avoid the buffets of life.

Info dude: Dr Pagoto's words quite clearly apply to internet porn as well. The obsession that is built into internet porn is not an obsession for seeing naked people. It is an obsession for novelty. Internet porn addiction is an addiction to novelty.

Dr speak (*Shwetank Bansal, Neuropsychiatrist, Sexologist, Delhi*): For example, if we restricted alcohol consumption to only once a week, don't you think that will completely remove the addictive element. The same way, in today's internet porn that element of restricted use is not there, it is available everywhere, all the time, at unlimited supply.

4) *Sensitisation. When you like it a lot, you tend to like it more and more.*

Info dude: So, you know addiction causes desensitisation. Well, it also causes sensitisation, meaning that the brain becomes wired in a way that it starts craving the addictive element more and more.

Dr speak (*Valerie Voon, Neuropsychiatrist*): When an alcoholic sees an advertisement for a drink, their brain will light up and be stimulated in a certain way. We are seeing this same kind of activity in users of pornography.

Dr speak (*John Dani, Neuroscientist*): When specific environmental events occur, such as the place or people associated with drug use, they are capable of cuing drug-associated memories or feelings that motivate continued drug use or relapse.

Info dude: Regular porn use can form this deeply embedded memory of pleasure. The brain associates watching porn to gaining pleasure, so it starts associating all the things that happen around the act of watching porn as a cue to getting that lovely bust of dopamine through porn. So, when you turn on your computer, open the internet browser, or do any of these things that you would do when watching porn, the embedded memory kicks in and starts craving pornography. Your brain wants that hit of dopamine, and it does whatever it takes, to get it. This can make the addiction more compelling than other activities in the addict's life.

Are you wondering how common this porn addiction thing is?

My man **Kanye West**, the guy who is married to a woman most men fantasise about on a regular basis, is, yes, addicted to porn. He has been quoted as saying, 'My only drug is porn'.[143]

John Mayer, yes that good-looking singing sensation, who has dated the likes of Katy Perry, Taylor Swift, Jennifer Aniston, Jessica Simpson, and so on, has often acknowledged how his porno habit has often gotten out of hand: 'There have probably been days when I saw 300 vaginas before I got out of bed,' Mayer told *Playboy* in an interview in 2010.

He went on to say that pornography has ruined his generation's expectations of relationships.

'You're looking for the one photo out of 11 you swear is going to be the one you finish to, and you still don't finish,' he said. 'How does that not affect the psychology of having a relationship with somebody? It's got to.'

Even the best golfer to ever play the game, **Tiger Woods**, who also happens to be one of the richest sportsmen on the planet, has been reported to have had his phone and hotel rooms loaded with porn. Porn addiction?[144]

The American actor/director/former football player, Terry Crews, has quite openly spoken about how pornography addiction was destroying his life and had almost ended his marriage. 'My wife was literally like, "I don't know you anymore, I'm out of here." Pornography is a major, major problem, I literally had to go to rehab for it.'[145]

If these handsome, rich, famous men, who can have orgies at will with the hottest women on the planet, can manage to get addicted to porn, anyone of us can. Period!

Confirmed sceptic: Hmmm, fascinating dude. I must say, you have made me think and not be sceptical about something for a change. Tell me, how can someone know if they are edging towards porn addiction?

Info dude: Ah, Mr Sceptic, you will make me cry. Now, how can one check if they have a full-blown addiction to porn? (Remember, you could be only partially bordering towards addiction and it would still be seriously messing things in your life.). Let's listen in on Dr Manoj Kumar from the one and only Clinic for Technology Addiction in India (we need more such clinics).

Dr speak (*Manoj Kumar, Psychiatrist, Technology Addiction, Bangalore*): We have developed a five-C criteria to check for addiction:

a) Craving: If you have a continuous desire to consume something.

b) Control: Whenever you feel you are losing control when indulging in any activity or substance.

c) Coping: When you start using an activity or substance as a coping mechanism. To deal with stress, boredom etc.

d) Compulsion: Is it becoming a compulsive habit? There are other activities you should be doing but you want to keep indulging in this behaviour or substance.

e) Consequences: Are you experiencing negative psychological, social, physical, societal consequences due to this behaviour?

If out of these, four Cs are ticked, then the person is addicted to the substance or behaviour.

There are also many pornography addiction screening tests online. You can take those tests.

Dr speak (*Ajay Nigalani, Neuropsychiatrist, Sexologist, Delhi*): Can internet porn be addictive? Yes, it can. You have to be the judge if it is having an effect on your life. If it is, then you are crossing a line.

Info dude: So, if this porn stuff has started messing with your relationships or your libido or your head in any way at all, then turn to the next chapter. If any form of addiction is messing with you, then turn to the next chapter. If you simply want to know how does one deal with addiction (of any kind), to help yourself or someone else, then turn to the next chapter. If not, then skip the next chapter and keep reading. We will talk about banning things, always a fun topic.

13

It's Messing with Me, Now What?

'The store sells phones that cannot connect to a WiFi, laptops that don't have any screen, tablets that self-destruct every time you search for porn. Pure porn vegan bliss!'

> *'I heard that internet addiction is now an official mental disorder and you can go to rehab for it. I'm only going if there is WiFi.'*
>
> *—Unknown*

The Science of Dealing with Porn Addiction

Dr speak (*Manoj Kumar, Psychiatrist, Technology Addiction, Bangalore*): First, you must acknowledge that porn is becoming a problem in your life.

Info dude: Because to fix a problem, you must first accept that the problem exists. If your dog goes around biting people, then you must first stop saying 'My cute little puppy is harmless', because no, it is not. Your puppy has grown into a vicious dog who bites people; now, you can start looking at ways to fix the problem. So, you must first accept that viewing internet porn is messing with you.

Now, let's start fixing it.

The first step towards regaining control is to give your brain a rest from all artificial sexual stimulation for several months. Stop watching porn—no porn whatsoever. Among other things, this will help you establish what impact pornography was having on you.

Dr speak (*Sharmila Majumdar, Sexologist, Hyderabad*): People who are being negatively impacted by it, need to cut off all options to watch porn completely.

Clinical reports suggest that terminating internet pornography use is sometimes sufficient to reverse negative effects.[146]

This process is also called 'rebooting'. It's a way of rediscovering what you are like without porn in your life. The idea is that by avoiding artificial sexual stimulation you are shutting down and restarting the brain, rebooting it. Returning it to its default setting.

Now, shutting off completely from porn will be tricky for most people. The severity of withdrawal symptoms can catch people who try to suddenly go off porn by surprise.

A study in 2013 reported that internet addicts suffer a form of cold turkey when they stop using the Web, just like people coming off substance drugs.[147]

So if you can, then stop watching porn altogether. After six months, see how it has impacted your life and then take a call on whether you want to go back to it (see the chapter 'Good Porn'). If cold turkey is not happening, or you are simply not able to do it, then, well then read on.

Dr speak (*Manoj Kumar, Psychiatrist, Technology Addiction, Bangalore*): The viewer who is having problems with excessive porn must first try fixing any lifestyle dysfunctions. Regulate their sleep, eat healthy, workout, etc. Once they improve their lifestyle, the pornography use should decrease automatically.

Case in point—The Rat Park[148]

A normal rat cage, in which rats are kept for experiments, is usually a box large enough to easily accommodate the rat, often soundproof and light-proof. Hundreds of trials have showed that lab rats readily became slaves to drugs such as heroin, cocaine, and amphetamines when the experiments are done in a rat cage. In 1976, the scientist Bruce Alexander decided to run a special experiment. He suspected that the problem with the drug experiments was the cage itself.

To test that hypothesis, Alexander built a paradise for rats. Rat Park was a plywood enclosure the size of 200 standard cages. There were all kinds of rat goodies—boxes, tin cans for hiding and nesting, poles for climbing, and plenty of food. Most important, because rats live in colonies, Rat Park housed 16 to 20 animals of both sexes.

Alexander then gave rats in the Rat Park and control animals in standard laboratory cages access to two water bottles, one filled with plain water and the other with morphine-laced water. The residents of the Rat Park overwhelmingly preferred plain water to morphine (over 99.9 percent of them). While the rats in the skinnier boxes preferred to get high on morphine.

In a variation he calls 'Kicking the Habit', Alexander gave rats in both the environments nothing but morphine-laced water for 57 days, until they were physically dependent on the drug. But as soon as they had a choice between plain water and morphine, the animals in the Rat Park switched to plain water more often than the caged rats did, voluntarily putting themselves through the discomfort of withdrawal to do so.

The Rat Park showed that a rat's environment, not the availability of drugs, leads to dependence. In a normal setting, a narcotic is an impediment to what rats typically do: fight, play, forage, mate. But a caged rat can't do those things. It's no surprise that a distressed animal with access to narcotics would use them to seek relief.

Info dude: It is important to point out that when it comes to humans, this experiment has its limitations, and there are many other factors that go into human addiction. The drug itself has a large part to play in it. But, this experiment does uderline the importance of having a vibrant, fulfilling life in order to beat an addiction.

Dr speak (*Manoj Kumar, Psychiatrist, Technology Addiction, Bangalore*): Users should engage themselves in other stimulating activities, because they have to replace the stimulation from porn with some healthy, stimulating activity.

Info dude: And what could be healthier than exercising, right? Exercising can fix desensitisation of dopamine caused by pornography (or any addiction).

Endurance training affects dopamine receptor binding and dopamine metabolite levels.[149]

Data indicate that chronic exercise decreases the positive-reinforcing effects of cocaine and support the possibility that exercise may be an effective intervention in drug-abuse prevention and treatment programs.[150]

Exercise can even help improve erectile dysfunctions that might be caused by porn.

It was demonstrated that increased physical activity is associated with better sexual function.[151]

Info dude: Step away from all those screens and go spend time in nature. It can improve prefrontal cortex functioning that gets negatively impacted by the superstimulus of internet porn.

Attention Restoration Theory (ART) suggests that exposure to nature can restore prefrontal cortex-mediated executive processes such as selective attention, problem solving, inhibition and multi-tasking.

Spending time in the nature can help you come up with more creative solutions to your problems.[152]

In an experiment, it was shown that four days of immersion in nature, and the corresponding disconnection from multimedia and technology, increased performance on a creativity, problem-solving task by a full 50 percent in a group of hikers.

The researchers anticipate that this happens because nature is emotionally positive and low-arousing, unlike the over stimulated world we live in.

Nature helps your brain function better, it works more in sync.

Using brain scanning that measures brain activity they showed that the natural, tranquil scenes caused different brain areas to become 'connected' with one another—indicating that these brain regions were working in sync.[153]

Info dude: Meditate. There is growing evidence that meditation helps us in taking better decisions, it helps us keep calm, and it helps us make better choices in our day-to-day life.

Meditation practice has been shown not only to benefit higher-order cognitive functions but also to alter brain activity.

Using high-resolution MRI data of 44 subjects, researchers detected more brain matter in the part of the meditator's brain that regulates emotion, and controls our responses.[154]

Info dude: All this while, keep trying to taper off your porn use, with the eventual goal of going completely off it. Watch out for 'triggers' that can drag you back to binging on porn.

Triggers are what addiction experts call 'cues'. How do they work? Your brain makes connections between the reward circuitry and any activity that rewards it (watching porn). Anything that activates these pathways is a 'cue', or trigger (turning on your computer, opening the browser and so on, these cues tell your brain that the rewarding activity of watching porn is about to happen).

In drug addicts, the cue-induced spike (of dopamine) can be as high as the spike from actually taking the drug.[155]

Dr speak (*Manoj Kumar, Psychiatrist, Technology Addiction, Bangalore*): We find that in porn addicts, there is a lot of resistance towards the treatment. Gaming addicts respond quite early on to treatment, but with porn addicts the treatment has to be slow and steady.

Info dude: If the struggle is getting too hard, remember that you are not alone, and go see a doctor.

Dr speak (*Ajay Nigalani, Neuropsychiatrist, Sexologist, Delhi*): Every psychiatrist has patients suffering from pornography's negative impact. Patients who get only excited by porn and the real thing does not excite them anymore, to people completely addicted to it—we get all variations of patients these days.

If you feel it is getting out of hand and impacting your life in negative ways, you should seek help. Starting with a mental health expert might be the best step.

Dr speak (*Sharmila Majumdar, Sexologist, Hyderabad*): One thing I would like to tell you is that pornography definitely has a negative effect on people's sexuality.

So many people who are suffering with pornography use come to me—people should meet a sexologist or a psychoanalyst, and sort this thing out. Pornography is definitely a negative influence.

Confirmed sceptic: Considering all the negative aspects, shouldn't we just ban all pornography?

Info dude: Should we?

14

Porn Ban!

Should We Ban Porn?

Cultured prude: Of course, we should ban porn. This whole book is proof that porn can be extremely harmful, so why not simply ban it?

Confirmed sceptic: I don't know, haven't we already tried doing that?

In July 2015, India's telecom ministry ordered internet service providers to block access to 857 websites hosting pornographic content.

But the government had clearly not predicted the scale of backlash that came their way. There were online campaigns, debates in the news and social media and a huge uproar—the message was clear, India was not okay with this ban.

A week later, the government backtracked. A new order was released that asked the service providers to block access only to those sites which have child pornographic content.

Info dude: The idea of banning pornography gets extreme reactions from people. Banning pornography after all is akin to moral policing, something people like Sir Culture here would endorse. At the risk of being labelled as a cultured prude myself, I must first state the following:

Going by all the scientific evidence and the fact that kids today have access to internet porn at the click of a button, porn ban seems like a completely legitimate option. To protect our kids from extremely damaging content should be our number-one priority at all times. We as a society completely accept the banning of crime, or murder, to yell 'fire' or 'bomb' is banned in public places, for very good reason, we accept the ban on provocative hate speech in public, because it can lead to harmful consequences. We have banned the use of certain drugs, we have banned the sale of alcohol or cigarettes to minors, all because these substances are harmful. So to ban Tube Porn websites which are proven to have a damaging impact on both adults and adolescents does not seem like a bad idea at all.

Having said this, here is why banning pornography is a bad idea!

1) Who decides what to ban?

Info dude: Porn is a lose term. Not all sex scenes are porn, not all porn has sex scenes in it. What do we ban? Will the ban end up shutting off all visual depictions of sex? That is definitely not cool and should be unacceptable.

2) No one controls the internet.

Info dude: Case in point, China!

Porn is strictly forbidden in China. While forbidding porn is one thing, actually getting rid of it is quite another, especially when users have social media, cloud-based services, and new payment methods at their disposal. Despite an ongoing crackdown against 'spiritual pollution', as the Communist Party once called it, porn is alive and thriving on China's internet.

Censors have closed down many services in recent years, but in a constant game of cat and mouse, providers and users have found other ways to share adult content, whether it's self-made or pirated from different studios.

3) Forbidden things turn us on even more.

Interestingly, forbidden activities can be unnaturally arousing. Dopamine rises sharply—especially in teens—when anticipating doing something novel or taking a risk, including doing something forbidden. This dopamine spurt urged our adolescent ancestors to risk embarking for new territories and avoid inbreeding. This makes, 'forbidden fruit taste the sweetest'.

Info dude: All in all, banning porn does not help anyone.

Dr speak (*Sharmila Majumdar, Sexologist, Hyderabad*): See, banning anything is not a solution, because it doesn't work. In fact, if it is banned it might be more easily available.

Dr speak (*Paras Shah, Sexologist, Ahmedabad*): No, the government already tried and they failed. The government cannot ban porn, it is not possible. People will find a way to watch it, all over the world, everyone is watching it. Pornography is more common than the common cold.

Every day thousands of new pornography sites are coming up, how many sites will they ban?

Confirmed sceptic: Damn, then what? We just let porn hijack our sexuality? And what about our kids? Dear lord, what about their adolescent brains?

Info dude: Mr Sceptic, you didn't think I will bring you this far in the book and then leave you without solutions, did you? Because I won't. Read on.

15
Advice for Parents

'Okay, so if babies come from God, is that why they call it the missionary position?'

The Solution

Info dude: Internet has changed the way our kids learn, grow and experience the world. If you are any older than 25, you probably feel quite dumb when you meet a kid today. Jesus, I was eating mud at that age, and this kid can order food on a phone. While the internet and other gadgets are having an immense positive impact on the world, do you honestly think this new reality the kids are now growing up in has no negative sides to it?

A study done with Chinese students found that within the first year, 40 percent of students who hardly used the internet before had developed a full-blown internet addiction.

Before they were addicted to the internet, the scores of depression, anxiety, and hostility for students were lower than the norm. After their addiction (one year later), the dimensions increased significantly, suggesting that depression, anxiety, and hostility were outcomes of internet addiction, and not precursors for internet addiction.[156]

Dr speak (*Phillip Zimbardo, Psychologist, TED Talks Speaker*)[157]: Arousal addiction (porn, video games) is a major factor in the increase in social awkwardness and anxiety among digital natives. Excessive screen time is interfering with the development of normal social skills.

More recently, Taiwanese researchers showed that there is a correlation between teen suicide ideation/attempt and internet addiction.[158]

Info dude: Today, kids access the internet and once an adolescent has access to the internet, Tube Porn is only a click away. We all know how that impacts an adolescent brain (see the chapter 'Kids on Porn'). But internet is an integral part of our lives today, this too is a fact. A lot of good comes from adolescents having access to it. Internet has also become an intrinsic part of the learning process in schools and at home, and its role is only bound to increase.

It seems futile to try and keep adolescents away from explicit material altogether and recklessly irresponsible not to educate them about its harmful effects. We need to talk to them, educate them and inform them on the topic.

Dr speak (*U. Gauthamadas, Senior Consultant in Neuro Behavioural Medicine*): What is more harmful than watching porn is parents coming out heavily on their kids for watching porn.

Earlier the accessibility to pornographic material was hard, and hence parental restrictions could be imposed to a certain degree. But today parental restrictions simply cannot stop a kid from accessing porn. And any attempt to impose parental restriction today only increases curiosity and an urge to go to the porn site.

Confirmed sceptic: Jesus, what the hell are we to do then, dude?

Info dude: Two words, Mr Sceptic, two words—SEX EDUCATION.

Dr speak (*Paras Shah, Sexologist, Ahmedabad*): See, India used to have sex education hundreds and hundreds of years ago. Walls of temples had sex education on them. But then eventually the priorities changed. A veil had been thrown over sex education and that veil has still not been lifted. If anyone tries to talk about sex education now, politicians and religious leaders oppose it.

And, while we adults discuss if sex education should be given or not, the kids are indulging in sex and getting informed about it on their own.

Info dude: Sex education works.

The evaluation of comprehensive sex education programs from around the world show that these programs do work. They can help delay onset of sexual activity in young people, reduce its frequency, it can reduce the number of sexual partners a young person has, and it can have the critical effect of increasing the use of condoms and contraceptives.

An Indian politician a few years ago had said the following about implementing sex education in schools. Sex education will, he had said, 'promote promiscuity of the worst kind, strike at the root of the cultural fabric, corrupt Indian youth and lead to the collapse of the education system and the decrease of virginity age'.[159]

Unlike what some such delusional political and religious leaders would have us believe:

> *The evidence shows that youth who receive comprehensive sex education are NOT more likely to become sexually active, increase sexual activity, or experience negative sexual health outcomes.*[160]

Info dude: The CBSE did try doing something on the lines of sex education in India.

Dr speak (*Aastha Sachdeva, Psychiatrist, Child Psychologist*): The CBSE has tried putting in an adolescents' education program. I was trained for it about ten years ago. We were supposed to educate other counsellors and spread it across in our school systems. It does touch upon sexuality and other life skill aspects that connect to sexuality. So the CBSE did try, but how much of it is being implemented, or being used in schools is still inconclusive.

The implementation depends on the monitoring that comes from the CBSE. Efforts are being made, but it is still not part of the curriculum. Just teaching about male and female reproduction system in biology class is not good enough.

Info dude: The Indian government's efforts are too little, too late and too slow. All this while that we wait and ponder, kids are getting their sex education from internet porn.

Some private schools in India are pro-actively taking the onus to impact sex education:

> *In Delhi's Sardar Patel Vidyalaya, age-appropriation education sessions are held in the presence of doctors and psychologists. Kids are taught about good touch/bad touch in class; they learn about changing bodies and personal hygiene in class 6; by the 7th grade, girls and boys are separately taught about dealing with puberty issues, such as masturbation and aggression.*
>
> *The Springdale School in Delhi has discussions during their assemblies on issues ranging from the 2016 Delhi gangrape, sex in Bollywood, to compassion and value systems. The school also trains its teachers to deal with*

questions about premarital sex, dating, family issues and so on.

Info dude: Such schools unfortunately are an aberration. The methods they are using need to be researched on and then adopted as part of the curriculum by each and every school. The government, schools, and teachers all need to come together in taking the subject of sex education very seriously, and we need to act fast.

In order to keep up with the radically changing information landscape, communities, schools, and some governments around the world are coming up with innovative ideas to keep the kids safe from and informed about the dangers of the internet.

 # Recently, a leading sexologist in Denmark called for pornography to be shown in the classroom. According to Professor Christian Graugaard of Aalborg University, it can help teenagers become 'conscientious and critical consumers' who are able to tell the difference between pornography and the reality of sexual relationships.[161] *(This might not necessarily be the right approach, more research is needed to determine if it is, but at least he is trying.)*

 # The first ever Social Networking task force was set up to fight the major threats that they observed in Europe and came out with many practical and potentially useful rules like, having separate protected social media accounts for kids.[162] *(Again, at least they are trying.)*

Info dude: Meanwhile, there is one form of sex education that need not wait for approvals, and permissions, that can help our hormonal adolescents to better understand sexuality right this moment.

Sex education starts at home

Dr speak (*Paras Shah, Sexologist, Ahmedabad*): Now when an adolescent first gets curious about sex, he or she is likely to ask their parents about it. But more often than not the parents ignore or shove off the question. In this eventuality, the kid might stop asking them questions about sex from then on and the parents might feel the kid has stopped thinking about it. But they haven't, the kid will then get that information from elsewhere, and quite possibly get incorrect or even harmful information.

Start early

Dr speak (*U. Gauthamadas, Senior Consultant in Neuro Behavioural Medicine*): The right age is when the child shows any kind of curiosity towards sexuality. So it will be different with different kids. If the parents wait for the kid to be of a certain age, then it might be too late.

Dr speak (*Paras Shah, Sexologist, Ahmedabad*): Sex education should start from the cradle. To discuss and talk about everything connected to sexuality is sex education, not just how to have sex.

Dr speak (*Aastha Sachdeva, Psychiatrist, Child Psychologist*): It should be slowly introduced at an early age, just like talking about menstrual cycle, and other topics. We don't necessarily need to start talking about sex. You have to start making the kids sensitive to certain facts. Like a psychologist friend of mine told her son about the menstrual cycle at a young age and told him you are not supposed to make fun of a girl about such things. 'How would you like it if someone made fun of your mother and sister if our clothes are stained? So your approach when dealing with girls should be how you would want people to react to your mother and sister,' she told him. Biology classes do start at a young age but they don't talk about the socio-cultural ramification of biology.

Be a friend, not just a parent

Dr speak (*U. Gauthamadas, Senior Consultant in Neuro Behavioural Medicine*): The right approach is rather difficult for most parents. The right approach is to not be a parent but a friend. To be very open, encourage open discussions of everything without censorship, without judgment. This will enable the child to shed all inhibitions in discussing sexual feelings, sexual orientation, sexual urges with the parents. But that is a very hard task.

Dr speak (*Sharmila Majumdar, Sexologist, Hyderabad*): The parents have to be more friendly with their kids, and have to be in tune with their day-to-day activities.

Dr speak (*Aastha Sachdeva, Psychiatrist, Child Psychologist*): One important factor is not just how a parent brings about a discussion about sexuality, but how parents connect to the kid even otherwise.

I have had a student, whose mom is divorced and has a sexual partner and the child is completely in acceptance with this situation. That is an understanding a parent has to develop over time. The mother has been very supportive of the child at every step. So how you connect with your child is very important. Connect holistically.

Be aware of their activities

Dr speak (*Aastha Sachdeva, Psychiatrist, Child Psychologist*): First, we have to build awareness in parents about acceptance that kids these days have access to internet in one way or another, that kids are technologically more advanced than the parents themselves. So, the parents need to be themselves technologically aware of the websites and loopholes as to how a child can access explicit content.

Dr speak (*Ajay Nigalani, Neuropsychiatrist, Sexologist, Delhi*): First and foremost, have a continuous, warm relationship with your child. Being aware of your child's activities, be it their friend circle or social circle, also keep an eye on the material they are able to access.

Restrict access to the internet

Dr speak (*Aastha Sachdeva, Psychiatrist, Child Psychologist*): Parents also need to be smart about how to protect kids from explicit content (Firewall, tools to block explicit content on computers, etc.), not so they don't access it, but more because they don't stumble upon it. It is about limiting negative content and guiding their time and energy towards productive paths. And sometimes kids need to be guided in case they are getting very distracted. At times you might need to withdraw certain privileges as a tool to guide them.

Dr speak (*Sharmili Majumdar, Sexologist, Hyderabad*): Parents leaving kids alone with devices is dangerous. Sometimes kids are on their own with devices all day long. It can get too late very fast, they could watch pornography and get into unhealthy sexual contact, and then they come to us doctors with physiological and psychological impact, what are we supposed to do then? It is so difficult for us to then reinstate the previous state of mind, it is almost impossible.

Notice the symptoms

Dr speak (*Aastha Sachdeva, Psychiatrist, Child Psychologist*): In 2003, a 13-year-old girl, studying in grade eight, was complaining about not being able to concentrate in the class. After a few sessions I found out that the girl was attracted to a boy who was not responding positively and that's why she was having trouble concentrating in class.

Kids usually start showing certain signs and symptoms. I had a case once where the kid would feel drowsy in school, no matter what class it was. So in such cases you have to be vigilant as to why that might be happening. Are they watching porn late at night? Are they talking on the phone late at night? Has there been a recent change in passwords of their accounts? All these are alert signs. Other kids are the ones who would tell me how they access porn through incognito window. Now, why would a kid ever need to use the incognito window? Why do they have to be secretive at 11 pm?

Answer their questions, or find out how to

Dr speak (*Paras Shah, Sexologist, Ahmedabad*): If your kid asks you a question you are not sure how to answer, you should simply ask the kid for some time. Tell them 'I will let you know by tomorrow' and discuss it with others or ask a doctor and then give them an informed answer. Never ignore their question or worse, scold them for asking one.

Info dude: Parenting needs to change with the changing times.

Dr speak (*Aastha Sachdeva, Psychiatrist, Child Psychologist*): Kids these days are much more open about sexuality. From my own experience, I have noticed that kids now will talk about sexual issues a lot more openly than the kids five or ten years ago did. Students these days quite openly tell me, during sessions, about their sexual experiences.

Info dude: If you suspect that your kid is already being negatively impacted by porn, go see a counsellor or a child psychiatrist immediately.

Dr speak (*Aastha Sachdeva, Psychiatrist, Child Psychologist*): The first step as a doctor/professional counsellor would be to analyse the impact pornography use is having on the child. Go into how widespread the impact is. The next step, according to me, would be to look into the case history, the lifestyle of the adolescent. Once that has been explored, one can work with both the family and the individual keeping in mind how much it would impact the kid if we include the family.

One needs to find out the sources of conditioning to that content, and then work backwards. You have to un-condition them, telling them 'stop watching, stop watching' will be of zero help. So, what needs to be done is schedule and structure the day, mutually together. That is done through certain behavioural techniques like reinforcing the person's positive behaviour, reducing the time they are spending watching pornography.

By using techniques like token economies, where the kid has to display enough positive behaviour in return of which they earn points which can then be exchanged with something they want. This is basically reinforcing behaviours that are productive in nature. Of course, it is more of a process of rehabilitation.

Info dude: It should be evident that educating kids about the negatives of pornography will not stop them from accessing porn. Teen brains evolve with a penchant for the weird and wonderful; they are powerfully drawn to novelty and surprise. Kids need an open, fun, and stimulating environment to lead a healthy and addiction-free lifestyle. They need to be able to discuss sexuality with adults in an open and safe environment.

Let's make our kids get some real sex education, let's work towards a home and school environment where the kids do not feel the need to go to a porn website to learn about sex. And even when they do end up watching that hardcore internet porn video, let's make sure they feel comfortable enough to come and talk to us parents and teachers about what they saw and how that made them feel. Let's make sure they are aware of the negative effects of porn and the fact that the sex they see on a porn website is an act.

More resources for parents/kids and discussions on the topic can be found at pornistan.in.

Now, is there such a thing as a safe porn website? Is watching porn ten minutes a day okay? Is there such a thing as 'good porn'?

16

Good Porn

'Arrey, no, no, no, you know I don't watch porn on Tuesdays and Fridays.'

Good Porn

Pornstar speak (*Marie and Jack Silva, Porn Actors and a couple*)[163]: After a shoot, during personal sex, I might do some weird thing you see in porn. Then one of us says, 'Wait, let's make real love.'

There's a wonderful playfulness to our personal sex. After sex at work, it's so nice to come home to the real thing.

Info dude: Internet porn is to sex, what looking at a photograph of a Ferrari is to driving one.

Dr speak (*Paras Shah, Sexologist, Ahmedabad*): Why do you go to watch a movie? Just to relax and have a good time. Once you come back to real life, you don't stay in the fantasy of that movie, or at least not for long. One can watch a pornography movie as entertainment, but should not bring that fantasy world to their real life. If one can maintain this clear distinction they can watch pornography without any problems.

But the problem is that due to lack of sex education, people are unable to distinguish between fantasy and real sex.

Dr speak (*Ajay Nigalani, Neuropsychiatrist, Sexologist, Delhi*): Is having a drink a good thing or bad? It depends on the amount. And the impact it has on your real life. Same goes with porn; if both the partners are enjoying it, then there is absolutely no harm.

Here is where it gets tricky though. With adult material there are categories, from the simple, good, adult fun to the averse to the ugly and, finally, to the dangerous. So where do you set the limit?

And the problem is that staying in just the good, adult fun is not a reality. Because everything is out there, and the tendency to explore will always be too attractive.

Dr speak (*Manoj Kumar, Psychiatrist, Technology Addiction, Bangalore*): Well, once at an emotional level you start enjoying watching porn, it will be very easy to start abusing it.

Confirmed sceptic: So what then, dude? Spill it out.

Info dude: Some research suggests that...you're not going to like this:

> *The results from a 2017 study done in England and Germany found that when the frequency of porn consumption reaches once a month, sexual satisfaction begins to decrease, and that the magnitude of the decrease becomes larger with each increase in the frequency of consumption.*[164]

> *Another research conducted in 2017 demonstrated that pornography use of less than 'once a month' has little or no impact on the sexual satisfaction (with the actual partner). Once viewing reaches once a month, a reduction in satisfaction initiates and any additional increases in viewing leads to a disproportionately larger decrease in satisfaction.*[165]

Info dude: Once a month or even less seems to be the sweet number. The superstimulus Tube Porn is obviously the kind of porn with the most negative side effects. One might be able to read erotica or look at static images much more frequently without any impact whatsoever. Also, how much porn will start impacting someone negatively will vary dramatically from person to person.

Dr speak (*Manoj Kumar, Psychiatrist, Technology Addiction, Bangalore*): I would say even if you want to watch any kind of porn only once, only do it if you are very confident that you can discipline yourself not to watch it again. If you have a doubt, then better stay away from it in the first place.

Info dude: As a matter of science, an attempt to sort good porn from bad might be futile. The brain's reward circuitry, which drives sexual arousal, has no definition of 'porn'. It just sends a 'go get it!' signal in response to whatever releases sufficient dopamine. For example, there are many sites producing female-friendly porn these days. Now, while that porn will have a lot less 'shock' value that comes with the violence in everyday Tube Porn, it will still supply endless dopamine to binge on, through the novelty effect. So, limiting your use of all kinds of easy to stream/access porn might be the best way to approach this.

Meanwhile, it might be best to explore other forms of porn—reading erotica, listening to erotic content, and the one form of pornography that is always available to us, our imagination. With partners, one can do role plays, read erotic content together, or just make up erotic stories and narrate them to each other. Once you get your imagination involved, the possibilities are endless.

Finally, the best way to look at porn consumption might be to always be aware that internet porn is a drug. You could have the drug occasionally, but you want to be very careful while using it. You always want to be cognisant of how it might be effecting you, you want to spend time going completely off it regularly, and you definitely want to keep the frequency of using that drug under check.

For healthy and fun ways to enhance your sex life, to explore your sexuality and for more discussions and resources, go to pornistan.in

17

The Future of Porn

The Future of Porn

Expert speak (*Gianluigi Perrone, Virtual Reality Producer*)[166]: Soon people will have access to every sexual fantasy or perversion that exists. We're trying to explore how to stimulate the senses in new ways that are not possible in nature.

Info dude: Porn has always been at the forefront of technological change. From VCRs to DVDs to Blue Ray to the internet, and now we have Virtual Reality (VR).

Expert speak (*Michelle Flynn, owner of an independent Australian production company*): I've been shooting the same sort of stuff for ten years. When I first put on a [VR] headset, my mind was blown. This is so important for the adult industry. You can break the fourth wall and really get involved.

Info dude: And the fourth wall it is breaking! Anyone who has ever tried VR knows how good it is at fooling the brain. Virtual Reality makes porn immersive, it makes it real!

Expert speak (*Eddy Olivares, Owner, Sex-toy Company*)[167]: The basic idea is to allow the brain to be tricked into thinking that the experience is real. When an actress comes close to you or when you initially look down at the action, your brain can be tricked.

Expert speak (*Brett Leonard, Director and Producer, Film and Music Video*)[168]: Virtual reality is a truly immersive medium and the level of graphics, already quite strong, will only continue to get better and better. You really feel like you are someplace else… and what you see, what you experience, impacts your brain. So there are major implications here, to societal structure, to democracy, to the way in which we interact with each other, to the nature of love, to the nature of sexuality.

Info dude: Remember how mirror neurons worked? Well, with Virtual Reality porn, the brain has no option but to think it is real. Although technologically only in its nascent stages, VR is already showing signs of the impact it will have in the near future.

One of the world's biggest pornography websites, *Naughty America*, has already seen more than 235,000 VR videos being downloaded by customers on its website, in a single month. A 60 percent rise in a single month for the number of VR videos being downloaded is not an aberration for the website.

'We help people find their fantasies, and VR brings our customers one step closer,' says Andreas Hronopoulos, CEO and owner of La Touraine Inc., *Naughty America*'s parent company. Virtual Reality is a significant and increasing revenue stream.'

From the time *Naughty America* released its first VR video, it has seen a significant rise in its revenue (27%); in 2016, its revenue due to VR porn was up by 433 percent.[169]

The world's most-visited porn website *PornHub* has revealed the number of people in the UK and Ireland watching its virtual reality content has risen 250 percent over the last year.[170]

Info dude: Virtual Reality in itself is a fascinating technology, and a lot is being done in different spheres of VR application. But pornography is clearly the one field where it is almost guaranteed to completely take over.

A UK-based virtual reality startup has released a standalone VR headset that works without a computer or a phone. Its VRotica headset only plays porn, and nothing else.

The company started selling the VRotica headset for $220 online recently, promising consumers access to triple-X-rated, 3D VR content.[171]

Info dude: This price range though already affordable, is likely to drop drastically in the next few years. There are VR headsets available in the market for as cheap as $20. Porn in the very near future is going to be about a lot more than just wearing Virtual Reality headsets though, it will also be about feeling the touch.

Expert speak (*Layla Savage, Virtual Reality Cam Performer*)[172]: Imagine you have a toy at home and while I run my finger along the one on my end, it vibrates the same way at your end. You get to experience what I'd do to you.

Expert speak (*Eddy Olivares, Owner, Sex-toy Company*)[173]: The toy we will make with VR porn in mind, will be a hands-free stroker for men that will use magnetic technology to perform the stroking action. This will synchronise with VR porn very well and remove the need for a user to physically move the toy. Fantasy will become realistic.

Info dude: Some users who have been using Bluetooth sex devices with webcam girls say 'they feel as if they're really there with her. One fan told a cam girl, the only thing better would be the ability to smell her scent'.

Smell might not be that far away in the future.

Dr speak (*Elina Berglund, PhD*): Future technologies, like advanced wearable tech, virtual reality, intelligent sex toys and artificial skin, will become part of our everyday lives and redefine the way we enjoy sex.

Info dude: These devices will obviously help out in some amazing ways. There is also a possibility that watching porn through VR might offset some of the negative impacts of internet porn.

Expert speak (*Michelle Flynn, Owner of an independent Australian production company*): It's really cool for people who don't identify with their own gender, and for people with disabilities. You can be in a body you're not physically in.

Complete immersion could mean there is not the disengaged, voyeuristic quality typical of traditionally filmed porn, potentially increasing sensitivity and empathy. If a scene is filmed from more than one perspective, there is the intriguing possibility of switching perspective and seeing everything from the other participant's viewpoint.

Info dude: While there are possibilities of good, the possibility that VR porn will magnify some of the negative impacts of internet porn is equally high. Virtual Reality will be exactly that, it will not be reality. The superstimulant powers of internet porn will be magnified with technologies like VR. But then again, it is not VR that is the problem here, just like with internet porn, the problem isn't the internet.

Expert speak (*Gianluigi Perrone, Virtual Reality Producer*): There are ethical issues related to VR, because it's about mind control. It will be a cage, a prison for many people. But then nuclear fission was supposed to be used to cure cancer; it's not [about] the technology, but the people behind it.

Dr speak (*Manoj Kumar, Psychiatrist, Technology Addiction, Bangalore*): It still has to be seen what happens with the use of new technology for porn. It could be a blessing for some people who have medical ED problems or it might help some people therapeutically. But for general public, if the current use is having a negative impact then the porn of future will only make things worse.

Info dude: The future of porn is bright. It will get more immersive and vivid. However, the future of our sexual health looks bleak. We need better sex education. We need to make ourselves and our kids understand the difference between real sex and virtual sex.

To form naturally healthy sexual habits, we need to have naturally healthy sexual thoughts and experiences. Porn of the present and more so the porn of the future, serve us best only as a one off entertainment activity.

There is an urgent need in India to educate our kids about sexuality. Anyone who wants to start a discussion, connect with others who are working in the field of sex education, connect with doctors who are working in the field of sex education, or get more information about how to approach the subject with their kids, can go to **'pornistan.in'**.

Pornistan.in also has videos on the topic, information about doctors from across India who can help in dealing with issues around sexuality, discussions for men, links to more recent studies which shed light on the impact of porn, and other resources.

References

Chapter 1

1. Ankit Gupta, 'Popularity of sex toys in India', desiblitz.com, Retrieved- Sep 2017, https://www.desiblitz.com/content/popularity-sex-toys-india
2. hindustantimes.com, 09/2017, 'Punjabi women buy most sex toys, sales go up during Navratri in Gujarat: Survey', http://www.hindustantimes.com/sex-and-relationships/punjabi-women-buy-most-sex-toys-sales-go-up-during-navratri-in-gujarat-survey/story-HCcJsa PWN05mcc89qy1ksL.html
3. Sarah-Louise Kearney, desiblitz.com, Nov 2017, https://www.desiblitz.com/content/punjabi-women-buy-sex-toys-india
4. Srijani Ganguly, indiatoday.intoday.in, March 2017, http://indiatoday.intoday.in/story/sex-toys-india-increased-sale-purchase-ban-adult-wellness-vendors-lifest/1/907476.html
5. Maria Thomas, qz.com, August 2015, Retrieved- Sep 2017, After the US and China, India is the third-largest market for morning after pills, Link: https://qz.com/472407/after-the-us-and-china-india-is-the-third-largest-market-for-morning-after-pills/
6. Ira Trivedi, *India in Love*, Aleph Book Company Pvt Ltd, 1st March 2014.
7. Consensus 2011. Government of India.
8. Fatima Bhojani, motherjones.com, JUN 2014, Retrieved-Sep 2017, http://www.motherjones.com/politics/2014/06/

sally-howard-the-kama-sutra-diaries-sexual-revolution-india/

9. Nu (De) Media: A Preliminary Study Into The Young Peoples' Access To Pornography Through The New Media. *Indian Streams Research Journal,* Vol. II, Issue. IV, DOI : 10.9780/22307850: http://isrj.org/UploadedData/975.pdf. Retrieved September 2017.
10. Gulveen Aulakh and Devina Sengupta, economictimes.indiatimes.com, June 2017, Plunging mobile data costs present a dirty picture, http://economictimes.indiatimes.com/articleshow/58967964.cms?utm_source=contentofinterest&utm_medium=text&utm_campaign=cppst
11. Shauvik Ghosh, livemint.com, Aug 2015, Retrieved- Sep 2017, Porn ban could cost Indian ISPs, telcos 30–70% of data revenue, https://www.livemint.com/Industry/VhuXq3jfADn2CrhK8nJ7pL/Oops-Indian-ISPs-telcos-could-lose-3070-of-data-revenue.html

Chapter 2

12. What is a neuron?, Retrieved- Sep 2017, https://qbi.uq.edu.au/brain/brain-anatomy/what-neuron
13. Lea Winerman, www.apa.org, Retrieved: 09/2017, The mind's mirror http://www.apa.org/monitor/oct05/mirror.aspx
14. Vilayanur Ramachandran, ted.com, November 2009, Retrieved- Sep 2017, The neurons that shaped civilization,, https://www.ted.com/talks/vs_ramachandran_the_neurons_that_shaped_civilization
15. Alison Motluk, newscientist.com, June 2008, Retrieved- Sep 2017, Mirror neurons control erection response to porn, https://www.newscientist.com/article/dn14147-mirror-neurons-control-erection-response-to-porn/

16. Dioner R.O, Khera A.M., Platt M.L., 29 March 2005, Retrieved- Sep 2017, Monkeys Pay Per View: Adaptive Valuation of Social Images by Rhesus Macaques, https://www.sciencedirect.com/science/article/pii/S096098220500093X
17. David J. Linden, vice.com, Feb 2015, Retrieved- Sep 2017, A Neuroscientist Explains Why We Look At Porn https://motherboard.vice.com/en_us/article/wnjka4/neuroscientist-david-linden-explains-porn

Chapter 3

18. wikipedia.org, https://en.wikipedia.org/wiki/History_of_sexuality_in_India, retrieved in September 2017.
19. Charukesi Ramadurai, bbc.com, Oct 2016, Retrieved- Sep 2017, http://www.bbc.com/travel/story/20150921-indias-temples-of-sex
20. Jason Overdorf, pri.org, May 2009, Retrieved- Sep 2017, Meet India's first porn star, https://www.pri.org/stories/2009-05-04/meet-indias-first-porn-star
21. pornhub.com, retrieved/pub January 2017, Pornhub's 2016 Year in Review, https://www.pornhub.com/insights/2016-year-in-review

Chapter 4

22. Kat McGowan, psychologytoday.com, Retrieved 09/2017, Dopamine, https://www.psychologytoday.com/basics/dopamine
23. Gary Wilson, *Your Brain on Porn*, Commonwealth Publishing, 25 August 2014.
24. Robert Sapolski, Feb 2011, Retrieved- Sep 2017, Talk at California academy of science, https://www.youtube.com/watch?v=axrywDP9Ii0
25. Susan Weinschenk PhD, psychologytoday.com, Sep 2012, Retrieved- Sep 2017, Why We're All Addicted to Texts-

Twitter and Google, https://www.psychologytoday.com/us/blog/brain-wise/201209/why-were-all-addicted-texts-twitter-and-google

26. Bridget M. Kuehn, Willingness to Work Hard Linked to Dopamine Response in Brain Regions, 2 MAY 2012, Retrieved- Sep 2017, https://newsatjama.jama.com/2012/05/02/willingness-to-work-hard-linked-to-dopamine-response-in-brain-regions/
27. Natalie Angier, 'A Molecule of Motivation, Dopamine Excels at Its Task', nytimes.com, OCT 2009, Retrieved- Sep 2017, https://www.nytimes.com/2009/10/27/science/27angier.html
28. Kevin Majeres, 'Harvard Scientist Explains what Porn does to your Brain', purityispossible.com, July 2016, Retrieved- Sep 2017 http://www.purityispossible.com/, http://www.intellectualtakeout.org/blog/harvard-scientist-explains-what-porn-does-your-brain

Chapter 5

29. wikipedia.org, Supernormal stimulus, Retrieved- Sep 2017, https://en.wikipedia.org/wiki/Supernormal_stimulus
30. Robert Krulwich, 'The Love That Dared Not Speak Its Name, Of A Beetle For A Beer Bottle', June 2013, Retrieved- Sep 2017, https://www.npr.org/sections/krulwich/2013/06/19/193493225/the-love-that-dared-not-speak-its-name-of-a-beetle-for-a-beer-bottle
31. Adam Benton, 'How old is the modern brain?', filthymonkeymen.com, Dec 2016, Retrieved- Sep 2017, http://www.filthymonkeymen.com/2016/12/07/how-old-modern-brain/
32. Lenoir M., Serre F., Cantin L., Ahmed S.H., 'Intense sweetness surpasses cocaine reward', -Aug 2007, Retrieved- Sep 2017, PLoS One. ;2(8):e698. https://www.ncbi.nlm.nih.gov/pubmed/17668074

33. Sarah Klein, 'Fatty foods may cause cocaine-like addiction', March 2010, Retrieved- Sep 2017, http://edition.cnn.com/2010/HEALTH/03/28/fatty.foods.brain/index.html

34. Krebs R.M., Heipertz D., Schuetze H., Duzel E., 'Novelty increases the mesolimbic functional connectivity of the substantia nigra/ventral tegmental area (SN/VTA) during reward anticipation: Evidence from high-resolution fMRI', Sep 2011, Retrieved- Sep 2017, Epub, 58(2): 647–55, https://www.ncbi.nlm.nih.gov/pubmed/21723396

35. Wittmann B.C., Bunzeck N., Dolan R.J., Düzel E., Neuroimage, 'Anticipation of novelty recruits reward system and hippocampus while promoting recollection', July 2007, 38(1): 194–202. Epub, https://www.ncbi.nlm.nih.gov/pubmed/17764976

36. Koukounas E., Over R., 'Changes in the magnitude of the eyeblink startle response during habituation of sexual arousal', Jun 2000, Retrieved- Sep 2017, *Behav Res Ther.*, 38(6). 573–84., https://www.ncbi.nlm.nih.gov/pubmed/10846806

37. Eideard, 'Pure Novelty Spurs The Brain', August 2006, Retrieved- Sep 2017, http://www.dvorak.org/blog/2006/08/28/pure-novelty-spurs-the-brain/

38. Sujal Pandey, 'How Big Is The Porn Industry?', MAY 2016, Retrieved- Sep 2017, http://www.howbigarethey.com/porn-industry/

39. Pharmanewsprwire, 'Plastic Surgery in India is on rise!, 9 September 2016, Retrieved- Sep 2017, http://pharmanewsprwire.com/plastic-surgery-in-india-is-on-rise/

40. timesofindia.com, Retrieved- Sep 2017, http://timesofindia.indiatimes.com/life-style/beauty/60-percent-rise-in-cosmetic-surgeries-ahead-of-V-Day/articleshow/50973674.cms

41. The rise of 'porn star' plastic surgery: Well-endowed celebrities and adult films are behind 40 per cent rise in demand for penis extensions says leading surgeon, May 2014, Retrieved- Sep 2017, http://www.dailymail.co.uk/femail/article-2643657/The-rise-porn-star-plastic-surgery-Well-endowed-celebrities-adult-films-40-cent-rise-demand-penis-extensions-says-leading-surgeon.html

Chapter 6

42. Suzannah Weiss, 'Here's the Difference Between Sex in Porn and Real Life', APRIL 2016, Retrieved- Sep 2017, https://www.glamour.com/story/porn-sex-vs-real-sex
43. A.V. Williams, 'Aussie porn stars reveal: What making porn taught them about sex', retrieved/pub Aug 2017, http://www.news.com.au/lifestyle/relationships/sex/aussie-porn-stars-reveal-what-making-porn-taught-them-about-sex/news-story/c4507626c6338519a4333f725f257a4c
44. Seymore Butts, 'Famous Porn Director Reveals the Jaw-Dropping Truth about Porn', Aug 2015, Retrieved- Sep 2017, https://www.menshealth.com/trending-news/a19547533/director-reveals-horrifying-truth-about-directing-porn/
45. Shutterstock, 'Porn Stars Reveal the Most Insane Things That Have Happened While Filming, BY Jun 2015, Retrieved- Sep 2017, https://www.menshealth.com/trending-news/a19547101/porn-stars-porn-crazy-sex-sex-accidents/
46. Catriona Harvey-Jenner, 'Weird questions about life as a porn star, answered by professionals', Retrieved/pub Jan 6, 2018, https://www.cosmopolitan.com/uk/love-sex/sex/ask-cosmo/a28888/porn-questions-answered-professionals-tanya-tate-joybear/

47. Gigi Engle, 'How the Normalization of Anal Sex Has Shifted the Conversation About Consent', Retrieved/pub Aug 2017, https://www.marieclaire.com/sex-love/a5489/rise-in-anal-sex-statistics/

48. Tanja Tydén and Christina Rogala, 'Sexual behaviour among men in Sweden and the impact of pornography', Oct 2004, Retrieved- Sep 2017, *PubMed*, 15(9): 590–93 https://www.researchgate.net/publication/8373887_Sexual_behaviour_among_men_in_Sweden_and_the_impact_of_pornography

49. Mary Rose Somarriba, 'The Porn Industry Is Abusive, and These Women Are Telling It Like It Is', Aug 2015, Retrieved- Sep 2017, https://verilymag.com/2015/08/porn-industry-playboy-mansion-sex-trafficking-belle-knox-rashida-jones-holly-madison

50. Word Pocket, 'Ask a Porn Star- "Do you have anal sex?"', Retrieved/pub Aug 2017, https://www.youtube.com/watch?v=2Z54gehPAyE,

51. Erich Goode, 'Moral Panics: The Social Construction of Deviance', 2009, Retrieved- Sep 2017, Nachman Ben-Yehuda, Wiley BlackWell.

52. Wendy Tuohy, 'Rougher, harder, violent: how porn is warping the male mind', July 2015, Retrieved- Sep 2017, http://www.dailytelegraph.com.au/rendezview/rougher-harder-violent-how-porn-is-warping-the-male-mind/news-story/504698ce318f551052847f13ac678fd1

53. thepinkcross.org, Retrieved Sep 2017, http://www.thepinkcross.org/porn-quotes/

54. Walker S., 'It's always just there in your face': young people's views on porn', Retrieved- Sep 2017, Temple-Smith M., Higgs P., Sanci L., *Sex Health*, Jun 2015, doi: 10.1071/SH14225.

55. Bonino S., Ciairano S., Emanuela, Elena, 'Use of pornography and self-reported engagement in sexual violence among adolescents', Jun 2004, Retrieved- Sep 2017,

https://www.tandfonline.com/doi/abs/10.1080/17405620600562359

56. Brown J.D, Kelly L. L' Engle, 'X-Rated Sexual Attitudes and Behaviors Associated With U.S. Early Adolescents' Exposure to Sexually Explicit Media', Feb 2009, Retrieved- Sep 2017, https://www.researchgate.net/publication/23654736_X-Rated_Sexual_Attitudes_and_Behaviors_Associated_With_US_Early_Adolescents%27_Exposure_to_Sexually_Explicit_Media
57. Tanja Tydén, Christina Rogala, 'Sexual behaviour among men in Sweden and the impact of pornography', Oct 2004, Retrieved- Sep 2017, https://www.researchgate.net/publication/8373887_Sexual_behaviour_among_men_in_Sweden_and_the_impact_of_pornography
58. Peter J., Valkenburg P.M., 'The influence of sexually explicit Internet material and peers on stereotypical beliefs about women's sexual roles: similarities and differences between adolescents and adults', *Cyberpsychol Behav Soc Netw*, Sep 2011, Retrieved- Sep 2017, doi: 10.1089/cyber.2010.0189.
59. Damayantti Datta, indiatoday.in/Confessions, Retrieved/pub March 2017, https://www.indiatoday.in/magazine/sex-survey/story/20170320-sex-confessions-men-women-india-today-sex-survey-985955-2017-03-14
60. kbcreativelab, 'Porn Sex vs. Real Sex: The Differences Explained with Food', July 2013, Retrieved- Sep 2017, https://www.youtube.com/watch?v=q64hTNEj6KQ

Chapter 7

61. Abigail Tucker, 'What Can Rodents Tell Us About Why Humans Love?', *Smithsonian Magazine*, February 2014, Retrieved- Sep 2017, https://www.smithsonianmag.com/science-nature/what-can-rodents-tell-us-about-why-humans-love-180949441/

62. Juan Velasquez, 'Why Prairie Voles Fall in Love: A Chemical Romance', February 13, 2013, Retrieved- Sep 2017, https://knowingneurons.com/2013/02/13/why-prairie-voles-fall-in-love-a-chemical-romance/
63. Why are pair-bonding tamarins and humans different from chimps?', Nov 2010, Retrieved- Sep 2017, https://yourbrainonporn.com/staying-in-love-monkey-style
64. Gary Wilson, 'Pair Bonding 101: Beware Novelty-As-Aphrodisiac', Youbrainonporn.com, retrieved -08/2017, https://www.yourbrainonporn.com/book/export/html/481
65. Jennifer Viegas, 'Flirty strangers sway how men see partners', *Discovery News*, March 2007, Retrieved- Sep 2017, http://www.abc.net.au/science/articles/2007/03/26/1881621.htm
66. Dolf Zillmann and Jennings Bryant, 'Pornography's Impact on Sexual Satisfaction', April 1988, Retrieved- Sep 2017, *Cyberpsychology, Behavior, and Social Networking*, Vol. 14, No. 9, https://onlinelibrary.wiley.com/doi/abs/10.1111/j.1559-1816.1988.tb00027.x
67. Doran Kirk, Price Joseph, 'Pornography and Marriage', *Journal of Family & Economic Issues*, Dec 2014, Retrieved- Sep 2017, http://web.b.ebscohost.com/abstract?direct=true&profile=ehost&scope=site&authtype=crawler&jrnl=10580476&AN= 99376650&h=OQcXF0MnF6gNQys7HoRu7WHy8leNJMxUZOy7DToI1mQmRGP6UOl1xoVrxUKAJiWq1DSKllSu6geNFwu5r5Nj6Q%3d%3d&crl=c&resultNs=AdminWebAuth&resultLocal=ErrCrlNotAuth&crlhashurl=login.aspx%3fdirect%3dtrue%26profile%3dehost%26scope%3dsite%26authtype%3dcrawler%26jrnl%3d10580476%26AN%3d99376650
68. Racidon P. Bernarte, Vincent Jude G. Estella, Dominador Jr. M. Nucon, Jin Danniel O. Villatema, 'Internet Pornography Consumption and Relationship Commitment of Filipino Married Individuals' Retrieved/

pub Aug 2016, https://www.yourbrainonporn.com/internet-pornography-consumption-and-relationship-commitment-filipino-married-individuals-2015

69. Perry S.L., 'Does Viewing Pornography Reduce Marital Quality Over Time? Evidence from Longitudinal Data', *Arch Sex Behav*, Retrieved/pub Feb 2017, doi: 10.1007/s10508-016-0770-y.
70. Paul J. Wright, 'Internet Pornography Exposure and Women's Attitude Towards Extramarital Sex: An Exploratory Study', April 2013, Retrieved- Sep 2017, Vol. 2, pp. 315–36, http://www.tandfonline.com/doi/abs/10.1080/10510974.2012.755643
71. Maddox A.M, Rhoades G.K., Markman H.J., 'Viewing Sexually-Explicit Materials Alone or Together: Associations with Relationship Quality', Dec 2009, Retrieved- Sep 2017, Retrieved- Sep 2017, *Arch Sex Behav*, Issue(2): pp. 441–48., doi:10.1007/s10508-009-9585-4.

Chapter 8

72. Vocabulary.com, Retrieved Sep 2017, https://www.vocabulary.com/dictionary/tolerance
73. Molly Soat, Social Media Triggers a Dopamine High, Retrieved - Sep 2017, https://www.ama.org/publications/MarketingNews/Pages/feeding-the-addiction.aspx
74. Johnson P.M., Kenny P.J., 'Dopamine D2 receptors in addiction-like reward dysfunction and compulsive eating in obese rats', *Nature Neuroscience*, March 2010, Retrieved- Sep 2017, https://www.reuniting.info/download/pdf/Johnsom.Kenny.Study.3.2010.pdf
75. Mrug S., Madan A., III Cook E.W., Wright R.A., 'Emotional and Physiological Desensitization to Real-Life and Movie Violence', Oct 2014, Retrieved- Sep 2017, Issue 5, pp. 1092–1108, doi: 10.1007/s10964-014-0202-z.
76. Koukounas E., Over R., 'Changes in the magnitude of the eyeblink startle response during habituation of

sexual arousal', *Behav Res Ther.* Jun 2000, Retrieved- Sep 2017, 38(6): 573–84, https://www.ncbi.nlm.nih.gov/pubmed/10846806

77. Kühn S., Gallinat J., Brain Structure and Functional Connectivity Associated With Pornography Consumption', *JAMA Psychiatry,* Retrieved- Sep 2017, 71(7): 827–34, https://jamanetwork.com/journals/jamapsychiatry/fullarticle/1874574
78. Frohmader K.S., Wiskerke J., Wise R.A., Lehman M.N., Coolen L.M., 'Methamphetamine acts on subpopulations of neurons regulating sexual behavior in male rats', *Neuroscience,* March 2010, Retrieved- Sep 2017, 166(3): 771–84, doi. 10.1016/j.neuroscience.2009.12.070.
79. Tania Luna, 'How a penny made me feel like a millionaire', July 2012, Retrieved- Sep 2017, https://www.ted.com/talks/tania_luna_how_a_penny_made_me_feel_like_a_millionaire
80. Robert Sapolsky, 'Dopamine Jackpot! Sapolsky on the Science of Pleasure', March 2011, Retrieved- Sep 2017, FORA.tv, https://www.youtube.com/watch?v=axrywDP9Ii0
81. Taryn Hillin, 'Science explains why surprise brings us pleasure', April 2015, Retrieved- Sep 2017, https://splinternews.com/science-explains-why-surprise-brings-us-pleasure-1793846784
82. Zillmann D., Jennings B., 'Shifting Preferences In Pornography Consumption', Oct 1986, Retrieved- Sep 2017, Vol 13, Issue 4, http://journals.sagepub.com/doi/abs/10.1177/009365086013004003
83. Wéry A., Billieux J., 'Online sexual activities: An exploratory study of problematic and non-problematic usage patterns in a sample of men', Dec 2015, Retrieved- Sep 2017, Vol. 56, pp. 257–66, https://doi.org/10.1016/j.chb.2015.11.046

84. Kathryn C., Rogers M., 'Does deviant pornography use follow a Guttman-like progression?', *Computers in Human Behavior*, Sep 2013, Retrieved- Sep 2017, https://www.researchgate.net/publication/257253220_Does_deviant_pornography_use_follow_a_Guttman-like_progression
85. Sharlene A. Wolchik, 'The effect of emotional arousal on subsequent sexual arousal in men', *Journal of Abnormal Psychology*, Aug 1980, Retrieved- Sep 2017, pp. 595–98, 10.1037/0021-843X.89.4.595
86. Barlow D., Sakheim D.K., Beck J.G., 'Anxiety increases sexual arousal', *Journal of Abnormal Psychology*, March 1983, Retrieved- Sep 2017, *92*(1), 49–54, DOI: 10.1037/0021-843X.92.1.49.
87. Emma Elsworthy, 'Bare truths about porn: Pornification of modern society is taking a toll on our sexual morality', Sep 2014, Retrieved- Sep 2017, https://www.theherald.com.au/story/2553854/bare-truths-about-porn/
88. Norman Doidge, 'The Brain That Changes Itself', April 2007, Viking Books.
89. Heather Saul, 'Lisa Ann discusses how the demand for extreme porn can damage new performers: "That does break you down as a woman"', Jan 2016, Retrieved- Sep 2017, https://www.independent.co.uk/news/people/lisa-ann-on-how-demand-for-extreme-porn-is-damaging-new-performers-that-does-break-you-down-as-a-a6838751.html#gallery
90. 'Porn Star Elizabeth Rollings Escapes the Killer Porn Industry', May 2011, Retrieved- Sep 2017, https://endsexualexploitation.org/articles/porn-star-elizabeth-rollings-escapes-the-killer-porn-industry/

Chapter 9

91. Lisa J. Cohen, 'Does sexuality differ for men and women?', Feb 2011, Retrieved- Sep 2017, https://www.

psychologytoday.com/us/blog/handy-psychology-answers/201102/does-sexuality-differ-men-and-women

92. Kayt Sukel, 'The Neuroscience of Porn Viewing', May 2013, Retrieved- Sep 2017, https://www.huffingtonpost.com/kayt-sukel/the-neuroscience-of-porn-viewing_b_2955650.html
93. Richard Sine, 'Sex Drive: How Do Men and Women Compare?', Retrieved- Sep 2017, https://www.webmd.com/sex/features/sex-drive-how-do-men-women-compare#1
94. Meuwissen I., Over R., 'Habituation and dishabituation of female sexual arousal', 1990, Retrieved- Sep 2017, Elsevier Ltd., 28(3): 217–26, doi.org/10.1016/0005-7967(90)90004-3.
95. Laan E., Everaerd W, 'Habituation of female sexual arousal to slides and film', *Arch Sex Behav.* 1995 Oct, Retrieved- Sep 2017, 24(5): 517–41, https://www.ncbi.nlm.nih.gov/pubmed/8561662
96. Joe Herbert M.B., 'A Surprising Hormone Is Important for Sexuality in Women', Jun 2016, Retrieved- Sep 2017, https://www.psychologytoday.com/us/blog/hormones-and-the-brain/201606/surprising-hormone-is-important-sexuality-in-women
97. Nigel Barber, 'Sex Hormones and Womanly Passions', July 2009, Retrieved- Sep 2017, https://www.psychologytoday.com/us/blog/the-human-beast/200907/sex-hormones-and-womanly-passions
98. Ira Glass, *Infinite Gent*, Retrieved 09/2017, https://www.thisamericanlife.org/radio-archives/episode/220/testosterone?act=2
99. Tanith Carey, 'Broken relationships. Zero self-esteem. Spiralling depression. The terrible price being paid by the young women addicted to porn', *The Daily Mail*, June 2017, http://www.dailymail.co.uk/femail/article-4582216/The-young-women-addicted-porn.html

100. Wright P.J., Arroyo A., Bae S., 'An Experimental Analysis of Young Women's Attitude Toward the Male Gaze Following Exposure to Centerfold Images of Varying Explicitness', Sep 2014, Retrieved- Sep 2017, pp. 1–11, doi.org/10.1080/08934215.2014.915048.

101. Susan M. Shaw, 'Men's leisure and women's lives: the impact of pornography on women', Dec 2010, Retrieved- Sep 2017, *Leisure Studies*, pp. 197–212, doi. org/10.1080/026143699374925.

102. Zillmann D., Bryant J.,'Pornography's Impact on Sexual Satisfaction', April 1988, Retrieved- Sep 2017, 18(5), pp. 438–53, doi.org/10.1111/j.1559-1816.1988.tb00027.x.

103. Wright P.J., Tokunaga R.S., Bae S., 'More than a dalliance? Pornography consumption and extramarital sex attitudes among married U.S. adults', 2014, Retrieved- Sep 2017, 3(2), 97–109, http://dx.doi.org/10.1037/ ppm0000024

104. Laier C., Pekal J., Brand M., 'Cybersex addiction in heterosexual female users of internet pornography can be explained by gratification hypothesis', *Cyberpsychol Behav Soc Netw.* 2014 Aug, Retrieved- Sep 2017, Vol. 1, Issue 8, doi: 10.1089/cyber.2013.0396.

105. Goldsmith K., Dunkley C.R., Dang S.S., Gorzalka B.B., 'Pornography consumption and its association with sexual concerns and expectations among young men and women', *The Canadian Journal of Human Sexuality*, Vol. 26 Issue 2, August 2017, pp. 151–162, https://doi. org/10.3138/cjhs.262-a2.

Chapter 10

106. India's urban children spend 4 hours on mobile internet per day: survey, Feb 2016, Retrieved- Sep 2017, http:// www.deccanchronicle.com/technology/mobiles-and-tabs/090216/india-s-urban-children-spend-4-hours-on-mobile-internet-per-day-survey.html

107. Ronald Kotulak, 'Teens driven to distraction', March 2006, Retrieved- Sep 2017, http://www.chicagotribune.com/chi-0603240140mar24-story.html

108. Beyens I., Vandenbosch L., Eggermont S.,'Early Adolescent Boys' Exposure to Internet Pornography', *The Journal of Early Adolescence*, Sep 2014, Retrieved- Sep 2017, Vol. 35, Issue 8, http://journals.sagepub.com/doi/abs/10.1177/0272431614548069

109. Coming of Age: Millennials, July 2015, Retrieved- Sep 2017, https://www.pornhub.com/insights/millennials-demographics-statistics

110. Randel J., Sánchez A., 'Parenting in the Digital Age of Pornography', Retrieved/pub Feb 2017, https://www.huffingtonpost.com/jane-randel/parenting-in-the-digital-age-of-pornography_b_9301802.html

111. 'Teen brains over-process rewards, suggesting root of risky behaviour, mental ills', University of Pittsburgh, Jan 2011, Retrieved- Sep 2017, https://www.sciencedaily.com/releases/2011/01/110126121732.htm

112. Tanya Lewis, 'Teen Brains Really Are Wired to Seek Rewards', Jan 2014, Retrieved- Sep 2017, https://www.livescience.com/42532-teens-brains-respond-strongly-to-rewards.html

113. 'Brain Maturity Extends Well Beyond Teen Years', TONY COX- host, Oct 2011, Retrieved- Sep 2017, https://www.npr.org/templates/story/story.php?storyId=141164708

114. Steinberg L., Graham S., O'Brien L., Woolard J., Cauffman E., Banich M., 'Age differences in future orientation and delay discounting', *Child Dev.* Jan 2009; Retrieved- Sep 2017, 80(1): 28–44, doi: 10.1111/j.1467-8624.2008.01244.x.

115. Jason G. Goldman, 'Why animals also seek teenage kicks', Dec 2012, Retrieved- Sep 2017, http://www.bbc.com/future/story/20121211-animals-that-seek-teenage-kicks

116. Deann Ware, 'Neurons that Fire Together Wire Together', Retrieved- Sep 2017, https://www.dailyshoring.com/neurons-that-fire-together-wire-together/

117. 'First Sex: Just The Science Please', Oct 2013, Retrieved- Sep 2017, https://yourbrainonporn.com/first-sex-just-science-please

118. Harper C., Hodgins D.C., 'Examining Correlates of Problematic Internet Pornography Use Among University Students', *Journal of Behavioral Addictions*, Retrieved- Sep 2017, Vol. 5, Issue 2, https://doi.org/10.1556/2006.5.2016.022.

119. Seigfried-Spellar K.C., Rodgers K., 'Does deviant pornography use follow a Guttman-like progression?', *Computers in Human Behavior*, Vol. 29, Issue 5, September 2013, Retrieved- Sep 2017, pp. 1997–2003, https://doi.org/10.1016/j.chb.2013.04.018.

120. Kathryn C. Seigfried-Spellar, 'Deviant Pornography Use: The Role of Early-Onset Adult Pornography Use and Individual Differences', *International Journal of Cyber Behavior*, 2016, Retrieved- Sep 2017, DOI: 10.4018/IJCBPL.2016070103.

121. Imogen Parker, 'Young people, sex and relationships: The new norms', Aug 2014, Retrieved- Sep 2017, https://www.ippr.org/publications/young-people-sex-and-relationships-the-new-norms

Chapter 11

122. Harish Iyer, '*Shubh Mangal Saavdhan* and erectile dysfunction: Why should masculinity be defined by libido?', Retrieved/pub Sep 2017, https://www.firstpost.com/entertainment/bollywood/shubh-mangal-saavdhan-and-erectile-dysfunction-why-should-masculinity-be-defined-by-libido-4017849.html

123. Subhadra Menon, 'Studies show one out of every 10 men in India is impotent', April 1998, Retrieved-

Sep 2017, https://www.indiatoday.in/magazine/cover-story/story/19980427-studies-show-one-out-of-every-10-men-in-india-is-impotent-826247-1998-04-27

124. Dickson E.J., 'Is Internet Porn Making Young Men Impotent?', Retrieved/pub Sep 2017, https://www.rollingstone.com/culture/features/is-internet-porn-making-young-men-impotent-w503299

125. Steve Kim, 'Common Causes of Impotence', Feb 2016, Retrieved- Sep 2017, https://www.healthline.com/health/erectile-dysfunction/common-causes-impotence

126. Wery A., Billieux J., 'Online sexual activities: An exploratory study of problematic and non-problematic usage patterns in a sample of men', *Computers in Human Behavior,* March 2016, Retrieved- Sep 2017, https://doi.org/10.1016/j.chb.2015.11.046.

127. 'The Dual Control Model - The Role Of Sexual Inhibition & Excitation In Sexual Arousal And Behavior (2007)', retrieved/pub Jan 2018, https://www.yourbrainonporn.com/dual-control-model-role-sexual-inhibition-excitation-sexual-arousal-and-behavior-2007

128. Janssen E., Bancroft J., The Dual Control Model: The Role Of Sexual Inhibition & Excitation In Sexual Arousal And Behavior, 2007, Retrieved- Sep 2017, *The Psychophysiology of Sex,* Bloomington, IN: Indiana University Press, http://www.indiana.edu/~sexlab/files/pubs/JanssenBancroft.pdf

129. Brian Y. Park, Wilson G., Berger J., *et al.,* 'Is Internet Pornography Causing Sexual Dysfunctions? A Review with Clinical Reports', *Behav. Sci.* 2016, Retrieved- Sep 2017, 6(3), 17; doi: 10.3390/bs6030017.

130. Giuliano F., Allard J., 'Dopamine and male sexual function', *Eur Urol.* 2001 Dec, Retrieved- Sep 2017, 40(6): 601-08., https://www.ncbi.nlm.nih.gov/pubmed/11805404

131. Steinberg E.E., Keiflin R., Boivin J.R., *et al.,*'A causal link between prediction errors, dopamine neurons and

learning', *Nature Neuroscience,* Vol. 16, Retrieved Sep 2017, pp. 966–73 (2013), doi:10.1038/nn.3413.

132. Wright P.J., Tokunaga R.S., Sun C., *et al.*, 'Associative pathways between pornography consumption and reduced sexual satisfaction', Nov 2016, Retrieved- Sep 2017, *Nature Neuroscience* Vol. 16, pp. 966–73, https://doi.org/10.1080/14681994.2017.1323076.

133. Izabella St. James, *Bunny Tales: Behind Closed Doors at the Playboy Mansion*, July 2009, Retrieved- Sep 2017, Running Press Adult.

Chapter 12

134. Addiction, Retrieved- Sep 2017, https://www.psychologytoday.com/us/basics/addiction

135. Christopher M. Olsen, 'Natural Rewards, Neuroplasticity, and Non-Drug Addictions', *Neuropharmacology,* Dec 2011, Retrieved- Sep 2017, 61(7): 1109–122, doi: 10.1016/j.neuropharm.2011.03.010.

136. Kris Gunnars, '10 Similarities Between Sugar, Junk Food and Abusive Drugs', Sep 2014, Retrieved- Sep 2017, https://www.healthline.com/nutrition/10-similarities-between-junk-foods-and-drugs#section

137. Voon V., Mole T.B., Banca P., *et al.*, 'Neural Correlates of Sexual Cue Reactivity in Individuals with and without Compulsive Sexual Behaviours', 11 July 2014, Retrieved- Sep 2017, https://doi.org/10.1371/journal.pone.0102419.

138. Meerkerk G.J., Van Den Eijnden R.J., Garretsen H.F., 'Predicting compulsive Internet use: it's all about sex!', *Cyberpsychol Behav.* Feb 2006, Retrieved- Sep 2017, 9(1): 95–103, https://www.ncbi.nlm.nih.gov/pubmed/16497122.

139. Negash S., Sheppard N.V., Lambert N.M., *et al.*, 'Trading Later Rewards for Current Pleasure: Pornography

Consumption and Delay Discounting', *J Sex Res.* 2016 Jul-Aug, Retrieved- Sep 2017, pp. 689–700, doi: 10.1080/00224499.2015.1025123.

140. Cheng W., Chiou W.B., 'Exposure to Sexual Stimuli Induces Greater Discounting Leading to Increased Involvement in Cyber Delinquency Among Men', Feb 2018, Vol. 21 issue 2, https://doi.org/10.1089/cyber.2016.0582

141. Johnson P.M., Kenny P.J., 'Addiction-like reward dysfunction and compulsive eating in obese rats: Role for dopamine D2 receptors', 28 Mar 2010. Retrieved- Sep 2017, *Nature Neuroscience* Vol. 13, pp. 635–41, doi: 10.1038/nn.2519.

142. Sherry Pagoto, 'What Do Porn and Snickers Have in Common?', Aug 2012, Retrieved- Sep 2017, https://www.psychologytoday.com/us/blog/shrink/201208/what-do-porn-and-snickers-have-in-common

143. Nicole Bitette, 'Kanye West, John Mayer, Charlie Sheen and other celebrity porn addicts', Feb 2016, Retrieved- Sep 2017, http://beta.nydailynews.com/entertainment/gossip/celebrities-addicted-porn-kanye-west-joh-article-1.2542501

144. Chris Yuscavage, 'Things We Really Wish We Didn't Know About Tiger Woods' Sex Life', May 2015, Retrieved- Sep 2017, http://www.complex.com/sports/2015/05/things-we-wish-we-didnt-know-about-tiger-woods-sex-life/

145. 'Why Terry Crews Wants You To Stop Watching Porn', Feb 2016, Retrieved- Sep 2017, https://fightthenewdrug.org/why-actor-terry-crews-wants-people-to-stop-watching-porn/

Chapter 13

146. Park B.Y., Wilson G., Berger J., *et al.* , 'Is Internet Pornography Causing Sexual Dysfunctions? A Review

with Clinical Reports', 2016, Retrieved- Sep 2017, 6(3): 17; doi: 10.3390/bs6030017.

147. Romano M., Osborne L.A., Truzoli R., 'Differential Psychological Impact of Internet Exposure on Internet Addicts', Feb 2013, Retrieved- Sep 2017, https://doi.org/10.1371/journal.pone.0055162

148. Rat Park, Retrieved- Sep 2017, https://en.wikipedia.org/wiki/Rat_Park

149. MacRae P.G., Spirduso W.W., Cartee G.D., *et al.*, 'Endurance training effects on striatal D2 dopamine receptor binding and striatal dopamine metabolite levels', *Neurosci Lett.* 1987 Aug, Retrieved- Sep 2017, 79(1–2): 138–44, https://www.ncbi.nlm.nih.gov/pubmed/2959886.

150. Smith M.A., Schmidt K.T., Iordanou J.C., *et al.*, 'Aerobic Exercise Decreases the Positive-Reinforcing Effects of Cocaine', *Drug Alcohol Depend.* Nov 2008, Retrieved- Sep 2017, 98(1–2): 129–35. doi:10.1016/j.drugalcdep.2008.05.006.

151. Hsiao W., Shrewsberry A.B., Moses K.A., *et al.*, 'Exercise is associated with better erectile function in men under 40 as evaluated by the International Index of Erectile Function', *J Sex Med.* Feb 2012, Retrieved- Sep 2017, 9(2): 524–30, doi: 10.1111/j.1743-6109.2011.02560.x.

152. Atchley R.A., Strayer D.L., Atchley P., 'Creativity in the Wild: Improving Creative Reasoning through Immersion in Natural Settings', 12 December 2012, Retrieved- Sep 2017, https://doi.org/10.1371/journal.pone.0051474

153. 'Study shows tranquil scenes have positive impact on brain', Sep 2012, Retrieved- Sep 2017, https://doi.org/10.1371/journal.pone.0051474, https://www.sheffield.ac.uk/news/nr/1739-1.174080

154. Luders E., Toga A.W., Lepore N., *et al.*, 'The underlying anatomical correlates of long-term meditation: larger hippocampal and frontal volumes of gray matter',

April 2009, Retrieved- Sep 2017, *Neuroimage*, 45(3): 672–78, https://doi.org/10.1371/journal.pone.0051474, https://www.ncbi.nlm.nih.gov/pubmed/19280691

155. Schiffer W.K., Liebling C.N., Reiszel C., *et al.*, 'Cue-induced dopamine release predicts cocaine preference: positron emission tomography studies in freely moving rodents', *J Neurosci.* May 2009, Retrieved- Sep 2017, 29(19): 6176–185, doi: 10.1523/JNEUROSCI.5221-08.2009.

Chapter 14

156. Dong G., Lu Q., Zhou H., *et al.*, 'Precursor or Sequela: Pathological Disorders in People with Internet Addiction Disorder', February 2011, Retrieved- Sep 2017, https://doi.org/10.1371/journal.pone.0014703
157. Philip Zimbardo, 'The demise of guys?', TED2011, Retrieved- Sep 2017, https://www.ted.com/talks/zimchallenge
158. Lin I.H., Ko C.H., Chang Y.P., *et al.*, 'The association between suicidality and Internet addiction and activities in Taiwanese adolescents', *Compr Psychiatry.* Apr 2014, Retrieved- Sep 2017, 55(3): 504–10, doi: 10.1016/j.comppsych.2013.11.012.
159. Isha Singh Sawhney, 'Indian politicians want no sex in sex education', Aug 2014, Retrieved- Sep 2017, https://scroll.in/article/672379/indian-politicians-want-no-sex-in-sex-education
160. 'Comprehensive Sex Education: Research and Results', Retrieved- Sep 2017, http://www.advocatesforyouth.org/publications/1487
161. 'Porn belongs in the classroom, says Danish professor, Helen Russel', March 2016, Retrieved- Sep 2017, https://www.theguardian.com/culture/2015/mar/16/pornography-belongs-classroom-professor-denmark

Chapter 15

162. Nitish Chandan, 'Minimum Age to Use Social Networks in India', January 2015, Retrieved- Sep 2017, http://www.cyberblogindia.in/minimum-age-use-social-networks-india/

163. Michael Castleman, 'The Real Problem with Porn: It's Bad for Sex', Aug 2012, Retrieved- Sep 2017, https://www.psychologytoday.com/blog/all-about-sex/201207/the-real-problem-porn-its-bad-sex

164. Wright P.J., Steffen N.J., Sun C., 'Is the Relationship Between Pornography Consumption Frequency and Lower Sexual Satisfaction Curvilinear? Results From England and Germany', *Send to J Sex Res.* retrieved/pub 2017 Jul, doi: 10.1080/00224499.2017.1347912

165. Wright P.J., Bridges A.J., Sun C., *et al.*, 'Personal Pornography Viewing and Sexual Satisfaction: A Quadratic Analysis', April 2018, pp. 308–15, doi: 10.1080/0092623X.2017.1377131.

Chapter 17

166. Richard Lord, 'The future of sex? VR porn all the talk at Hong Kong's Asia Adult Expo as filmmakers get excited over the immersive possibilities', retrieved/pub Sep 2017, http://www.scmp.com/lifestyle/article/2110173/future-sex-vr-porn-all-talk-hong-kongs-asia-adult-expo-filmmakers-get.

167. Mandy Stadtmiller, 'Virtual reality sex is coming — and the toys are already here', May 2015, Retrieved- Sep 2017, https://mashable.com/2015/05/29/virtual-reality-sex/#hpzqkJ52pGqW

168. Blake Harris, 'HDTGM: A Conversation with Brett Leonard, Director of *The Lawnmower Man*', Dec 2016, Retrieved- Sep 2017, https://www.slashfilm.com/brett-leonard-interview-the-lawnmower-man/2/

169. David M. Ewalt, 'Naughty America Is The Future Of Porn', retrieved/pub Feb 2017, https://www.forbes.com/sites/davidewalt/2017/02/27/naughty-america-is-the-future-of-porn/#518f0cb16f2c
170. Jeff Parsons, 'The future of porn? Virtual reality viewing up 250% in 12 months as Brits strap on newest accessory', retrieved/pub May 2017, https://www.mirror.co.uk/tech/future-porn-virtual-reality-viewing-10432879
171. Janko Roettgers, 'A First Look at VRotica, a $220 Virtual Reality Headset Just for Watching Porn', retrieved/pub June 2017, http://variety.com/2017/digital/news/virtual-reality-porn-vrotica-vr-headset-1202478721/
172. Aurora Snow, 'The Future of Porn Is Here and It's So Real You Can Feel It', retrieved/pub July 2017, https://www.thedailybeast.com/the-future-of-porn-is-here-and-its-very-hands-on
173. Mandy Stadtmiller, 'Virtual reality sex is coming — and the toys are already here', May 2015, Retrieved- Sep 2017, https://mashable.com/2015/05/29/virtual-reality-sex/#hpzqkJ52pGqW

ACKNOWLEDGEMENTS

There are hundreds of individuals, experiences and resources that have helped me in deciphering and then putting into words this complex topic.

One of the most important resources in my journey was the website and book *Your Brain on Porn*, written and managed by Gary Wilson. Gary is doing exceptional work and was extremely helpful when I approached him.

The doctors who are doing critical work in the field of mental and sexual health in India and took out time from their busy schedules to talk to me. Dr Sharmila Majumdar, Dr Shwetank Bansal, Dr Ajay Nihalani, Dr Aastha Sachdeva, Dr Manoj Kumar Sharma, Dr U. Gauthamadas, Dr Paras Shah, Dr Manish Jain, and Dr Indranil Saha, I am eternally grateful to you.

Author Ira Trivedi, thank you for writing the excellent book, *India in Love*, and letting me use quotes from the book.

I have to thank the following doctors, scientists, actors and authors for doing the amazing work that they are all doing in their respective fields and for being kind enough to let me use some of it for the book: Brett Leonard (director), Tania Luna (author), Michelle Flynn (director), Dr Kevin Majeres, Dr Deann Ware, Dr Sherry Pagoto, Sandra Aamodt (neuroscientist), Adam Glasser (former porn actor/director–Seymore Butts), David Linden (neuroscientist), January Elizabeth (former pornstar), and finally—one of the smartest and funniest scientists on the planet—Robert M. Sapolsky (neuroendocrinologist).

None of this would have seen the light of day if it wasn't for my agent, the great Suhail Mathur of The Book Bakers. He truly is great.

I am grateful to Dipankar Mukherjee and Readomania for recognising the relevance of the book. Readomania has been publishing some gems, and I am glad to be a part of that list. The editor of this book Indrani Ganguly—it was an absolute pleasure working with you. Your edits and suggestions have taught me a lot about writing.

I am grateful to the talented Vinay Vikram Singh Sir for taking out time for the illustrations. You are an absolute genius. And, Devrishi Sharma Sir, thank you for putting the finishing touch to make the illustrations look amazing.

Finally, let me get down to my friends and family, who were never given a choice to not help me through this journey. They were forced to endure poorly written drafts and panic-ridden phone calls.

Priyadarshini Kacker, you are the reason I stuck to my self-imposed deadlines when writing this book. You are the creative genius behind the title of the book. Without your insights, none of the illustrations would have materialised. Everything you do has a unique style, a unique touch to it. Anyone who is not following you on Instagram is seriously missing out. (@p.kacker)

Punti (Puneet Rajput) and Subhav Kher, you losers had a big part in shaping this book. For the first time in my life, I felt it wasn't a complete waste having you as friends.

Isha Sharga, Sneha Jackob, Abhimanyu Mehta, Shruti Choudhary and Niti Singh, the fact that you are all doing ten different things in life and still took out time to read and give feedback, makes you guys the official heroes of this book.

My brothers—Amit Joshi, Bharat Joshi and Narender Sharma—for always being there for me. Naina, you know you are my favourite person, right?

Rajan Joshi, Cheenu Joshi and my Nani for their unconditional support and love.

And to the three most important people in my life, my parents—Mala Joshi Sharma, Surender Sharma—and my sister, Prachi Gautam. Your love makes it possible for me to fear less.

ADITYA GAUTAM
2018